One Pan Wonders II

More Backcountry Cooking

By Teresa "Dicentra" Black

http://www.onepanwonders.com

For Maddy.

One Pan Wonders II ~ More Backcountry Cooking

Cover photo © 2012 by Teresa Black
Additional Photography by Teresa Black, Monte Dodge, and Steve Cain

Additional editing by Steve Cain

ISBN:
First printing April 2012

Table of Contents

Acknowledgements 5
Introduction 8
Menu Planning...................................9
Beverages.....................................15
Breakfast 25
Lunches 37
Snacks and Trail Mixes...........................48
Salads 57
Soups 65
Ramen 77
Breads and Sides 81
Dinners.....................................87
Dessert 111
S'Mores.....................................123
Kids 126
Glossary. 131
Online Resources 134

Acknowledgements

The people I need to thank has grown exponentially since my previous book went to print. I have sent hundreds of meals off to various trails to be tested and this work could not exist if it were not for all of my willing Guinea pig hikers.

First of course, is my wonderful husband, who has not only tested recipes along side me and our daughter, but tolerated my stinky hiker trash friends crashing on the futon. He may not understand everything I do when it comes to food and backpacking, but he always supports me. He is always quick to remind me "don't forget to take a photo of the food." He is also a willing taste tester. The dessert recipes especially have benefited from his help.

My father, who thinks I could do no wrong. Thank you for always supporting me and listening to me ramble about things you don't understand.

Team Osbourne (West, Buchannan, Baker). My second family. You are always ready to test anything I send your way. Dustin has been especially helpful in finding marketing venues that I may not have thought of. Thank you for your constant support and encouragement. Your enthusiasm parallels my own.

Olyhiker, may you be at peace. I miss giggling and singing with you on the trails. I like to imagine that you are walking along with me on my adventures. It is an honor to have known you. The Olympics are perpetually filled with your memory. Several recipes in this book you helped test and develop. I will remember you fondly when eating them.

Hoosierdaddy, even though you are a key element of the PNWH, you deserve special recognition of your own. You have never for a moment doubted me, even when I was doubting myself. You have always told me exactly what you think of my concoctions – and it hasn't always been good! This constructive criticism is priceless. However, I will never subject myself to the smashed peanut butter and jelly sandwich that you hold in such high regard. Thank you also for being my constant traveling companion and listening to me repeatedly say "No, he's not my husband."

Freefall, so much of what One Pan Wonders has become can be traced directly back to you. You took a chance on me, inviting me to speak at ADZPCTKO years ago. As a direct result, I have been assimilated into the community that I had initially scoffed at. I would not want to be anywhere else. I am eternally grateful that you helped me find my hiker trash family. I look forward to what the next turn in the trail may bring. I never in my wildest dreams thought One Pan Wonders would be this successful this quickly. You obviously saw a niche in the community that needed filling. I am thrilled to be "the food lady" for all the crazy hiker trash.

Special thanks goes to Warner Springs Monty, who is not only the pickiest eater I have ever met, but continues to challenge and inspire me at every turn. He is one of my biggest cheerleaders and the best "Booth Bitch" a girl could ask for.

To all of my recipe testers – the thru hikers, the PNWH posse, the Pickle Gulch Crew, my PCT tribe and beyond. If I have forgotten someone, which of course is inevitable, I apologize. Cookbooks and the recipes within them would be nothing without willing recipe testers. Thank you all.

All Good, Animal, Anish, Basil, Beeman, Big John, Blue Sage, Carol, Catzia, Chemical Burn, Chipmunk, Chuck Norris, ChuckD, Clutch, Dicey, Eyebp, Day Late, Deborah, Doug, Durante, Flashback, Ford, Foxtrot, Fozzie, Freebie, Freefall, Gypsy, Half Mile, HikerJer, Hiking Drew, Hoosierdaddy, Joe Anderson, GoBlueHiker, Jester, LameBeaver, Lint, LdyBlade, Lookout, Maddy Monkey, Mad Monte, Marmot Stew, Marzit, MsDoolittle, Neville, No Granola, Nymph, ObiTonyKenobi, OlyHiker, Ol'Zeke, Orygawn, Otter, PhotoDavid6, ProDeal, Quark, Rainrunner, Rooinator, Rumidude, Sarbar, Sasquatch, Slugman, SnowPeak, SoFar, Spindle, Splash, Squatch, Steve Climber, Stumbling Norwegian, Sugar Momma, Super Claw, Swimswithtrout, The Graduate, Tigger, Trailhead, Turtle, Warner Springs Monty, Weather Carrot, Woodswoman, Wycanislatrans, Wyoming

Thank you! Thank you! Thank you!

Introduction

Food should have flavor and depth. It should taste good and be satisfying. While testing many of the recipes in this book, I have found that if I can serve it to my hubby at home without complaint, it will work beautifully on the trail. We have eaten a lot of "trail food" dinners right in our own house.

Two things I always remember about my trips are the weather and the food. We have no control over the first, but total control over the second. Good food can often make the difference between a fun trip and a miserable one when Mother Nature isn't cooperating.

On one memorable trip, a friend had packed in homemade lemon bars (packed tightly in Tupperware so they did not get smashed) as an after dinner surprise. We were delighted! On another trip a different friend brought us cinnamon rolls from the Cle Elum Bakery. She hid them in her pack until we were making coffee in the morning. Bakery cinnamon rolls beat instant oatmeal hands down every time! I've had real ice cream on the trail in the middle of summer thanks to a clever hiking partner. These are the exceptions to the backcountry food rules, but it is those exceptions that make certain trips more memorable than others.

My favorite outdoor activity is eating. The beauty of hiking and backpacking is that you have to eat – a lot! All that up and down over mountains and hills burns up a lot of calories. The longer and more difficult the trip, the more calories you burn, so eat up!

Menu Planning

I combine both recipes and pre-made, store bought items when planning a backcountry menu. I write out a menu for each day, including snacks, so that I have the right amount of food. In addition, salt, pepper, olive oil and individually wrapped tea bags go into my food bag on every trip.

To help with future meal planning, keep written out menus of each of your trips and take notes after each trip. This will help you in future planning because you can see what did or didn't work and what foods you would have liked more or less of. It will also help prevent you from repeating food disasters; like when we forgot the oil for a pan of cinnamon rolls. What a mess!

Things to consider when planning a menu:

Length of trip
Difficulty of trip
Hiking Style
Local Restrictions
Weather
Water availability
Amount of time for cooking
Foods to avoid
Number of people you are cooking for

Length of the trip

For a three day, low mileage trip you can bring a feast. A ten day trip without resupply is going to require much lighter, less bulky food choices. On longer trips, weight becomes a major consideration.

One trip I remember fondly, is a three day trip out on the Olympic coast when my friends and I planned an Italian themed potluck, complete with fresh bread, salad and dressing, Chianti wine, pasta and several sauces. We only had three miles to hike to camp, so why not bring food that would make us happy? The next year we had a similar trip, but with an Asian theme, complete with egg rolls, barbecued pork, fried rice and other dishes. Don't be afraid to make it fun.

Conversely, when doing section hikes on the Pacific Crest Trail, I tend to go as light as possible without sacrificing too many calories. Those trips rely heavily on just-add-water (aka freezer bag cooking) type meals.

Difficulty of the trip

In general, the more challenging the terrain, the more calories you are going to need. However, you will want foods that are lightweight. Additionally, if you are covering heavy miles, it is not likely that you will want to fuss with an elaborate meal when you finally do reach camp.

On trips such as these, I plan for a lot of snacks throughout the day to help keep my energy levels up. Some of my favorites to tote along are beef or turkey jerky, dried mangos, trail bars, fruit snacks and peanut butter M&Ms.

Hiking Style

What is your hiking style? Have you thought about it?

You should.

If you like to hike from sun up to sun down, your menu is going to be considerably different from a backpacker who likes to break camp later in the day after a leisurely breakfast or eat an elaborate dinner while the sun is setting. Nothing is wrong with either style, but you should be aware of how you like to manage your hike so that you can plan your menu accordingly.

Local Restrictions

You need to check the local restrictions and regulations before you leave on any backcountry trip. Are bear canisters required in the area you will be traveling through? Is there a fire ban on for the time frame that you are planning your hike?

If you need a bear canister, you will want to plan your menu so that you so not have bulky, space hogging foods that will take up a lot of space in the canister. For example tortillas are a wiser choice here than bagels or English muffins. More calories in less space will be your ultimate focus here. There are a lot of ideas throughout this book that will help you achieve that.

If there is a fire ban, forget the idea of s'mores in camp and plan for a different dessert.

Weather Considerations

Snow camping is fun. So is hiking in the desert.

I am from Seattle, which means I often hike in the rain. It isn't a lot of fun to try and prepare an elaborate dinner in a downpour. Check the weather before you leave on any backcountry trip and plan your menu accordingly. Choose meals that can be prepared quickly and with minimal effort or prep time when the weather is adverse.

On winter trips, plan ahead, expecting everything you pack to freeze. Don't pack trail bars that don't stay soft in cold temperatures. They will be impossible to chew in freezing temperatures.

Be sure to include lots of hot drinks and instant soups on your menu so that you have something to warm you while doing camp chores. The extra calories will also help keep you warm at night. In addition, a little fat and protein (ie: a handful of nuts) will help keep you a little warmer while you sleep. Winter hiking and camping is great because you get to eat lots and lots of fatty foods with the excuse that they will help to keep you warm. And they do.

In the heat of the desert, where water to cook with may be limited, consider going stove-free for dinner. Many of the lunch recipes in this book also make excellent dinners. Wraps make excellent meals and the possibilities of what you can include in them is just about endless. Experiment and see what works for you.

Water availability

Water needs to be taken into consideration in the winter as well as the heat of summer. You will be using up valuable stove fuel if you have to melt snow to cook your dinner.

In the desert, water is limited for other reasons. Going stove free is an option to conserve water. Another option is to have dry camps. Cook your dinner where you find a beautiful, scenic spot for cooking, earlier in the day, where water is available, and camp where water is not available. If you "camel-up" an hour or two before reaching your camp for the night and having access to water at camp may not be necessary.

Amount of time available for cooking

If you know you will be rolling into camp as the sun sets, you most likely will not want to plan for a big elaborate dinner. Don't forget that in addition to dinner you also need to do camp chores – setting up the tent, filtering water. On these types of trips you want to keep your dinner menu simple and maybe plan for a more elaborate breakfast meal.

Conversely, if you know you will reach camp early in the afternoon, feel free to plan a complicated dinner, complete with a fancy dessert. You may even want to plan your trip so that you can have just that sort of menu on at least one night.

Foods to avoid

If your hiking partner hates mushrooms, you are not going to win any favors by serving them Mushroom Stroganoff for dinner. Are their vegetarians or vegans in your hiking group?

It is important to ask about food allergies if you are in charge of planning the backpacking menu for others. Anaphylactic shock is nothing to screw around with in the backcountry.

The beauty of preparing your own food at home is that you have 100% control over the ingredients.

Number of people you are cooking for

How many people are you preparing meals for? You can either do individual servings (like freezer bag cooking) or you can cook one large meal for everyone. Sharing group cooking gear is also nice. There's no need for five people to bring five different stoves if they don't want to.

Chapter 1 - Beverages

For beverages calling for powdered milk, feel free to substitute powdered soy, rice, almond or goats milk. Use less sugar when substituting almond milk, as it is already very sweet. These types of beverages also add calories and nutrition to your hiker diet.

Flavored drinks will help encourage you to get enough fluids. Cool drinks will help cool you off in hot weather and warm drinks will help warm you up in cold weather. Adding flavorings to your water can help mask the taste of chemicals or "flat" water that treated water can often have. There are lots of different powdered mixes available, but also try bouillon, powdered gelatin, tea bags and cocoa mixes.

It is easier to eat if you stay hydrated. I get fewer blisters on my feet when I stay hydrated. Drinking enough water helps the skin stay elastic.

Herbal teas make lovely trail "iced" teas. Simply toss a couple of your favorite tea bags into your water bottle. Let stand for 30 minutes and drink.

The smoothie recipes in this chapter double as portable breakfasts. Mix one up and you are ready for a meal on the go. Save even more weight by mixing them up in a freezer bag and ditching the bottle.

Coconut Ginger Smoothie
Serves 1-2

Shake shake shake! Make sure you rinse out your container right away after drinking this. It can be difficult to clean if you let the remainder dry in the bottle.

1 packet vanilla instant breakfast powder
¼ cup powdered milk
2 tablespoons coconut crème powder
1 teaspoon ground ginger

At home: combine all of the dry ingredients in a zip locking plastic bag.

In camp: add about 1 cup of cold water to a screw top container. Add the smoothie mix and shake until thoroughly combined.

Creamsicle Smoothie
Serves 1

This tastes like those little cups of orange sherbet and vanilla ice cream from my childhood.

1 packet vanilla instant breakfast powder
1/3 cup powdered milk
2 tablespoons instant orange drink mix

At home: combine the dry ingredients in a zip locking plastic bag.

In camp: add about 1 cup of cold water to a screw top container. Add the smoothie mix and shake until thoroughly combined.

Mocha Almond Breakfast Shake
Serves 1

1 packet milk or dark chocolate instant breakfast powder
1/3 cup powdered milk
1-2 tablespoons instant coffee

At home: combine the dry ingredients in a zip locking plastic bag.

In camp: add about 1 cup of cold water to a screw top container. Add the mix and shake until thoroughly combined.

Variation: use flavored instant coffee.

Cherry Vanilla Chai
Serves 1

2 tablespoons sweetened instant cherry drink mix
1 packet instant vanilla chai mix

At home: combine all of the dry ingredients in a zip locking plastic bag.

In camp: add the contents of the bag to 8 ounces hot water. Stir well and enjoy.

Coconut Chai
Serves 1

2 tablespoons coconut crème powder
1 packet instant vanilla chai mix

At home: combine all of the dry ingredients in a zip locking plastic bag.

In camp: add the contents of the bag to 8 ounces hot water. Stir well and enjoy.

Peachy Green Iced Tea
Serves 1

The powdered green iced tea mix is available at higher end grocery stores and Asian markets. The green tea cuts the sweetness of the instant iced tea.

1 packet unsweetened powdered iced green tea
2 tablespoons instant sweetened peach flavor iced tea mix

At home: combine both mixes in a zip locking plastic bag.

In camp: add the mix to 8 ounces of cold water. Combine well before drinking.

Coffee

One summer I was woken up every morning in the backcountry with "Water is hot! You can get up and have coffee now!" That never failed to rouse me out of the tent, as the sun was barely rising and way earlier than I would ever get up on my own.

I am a big coffee drinker at home and I refuse to give that up on the trail. I have tried just about every way to make camp coffee. It seems that everyday more instant coffee products are being introduced to the marketplace. Additionally, they are getting better. Some of them are even drinkable!

Mexican Coffee Mix
Serves 1

1 tablespoon instant coffee (or more to taste)
1 teaspoon powdered milk
1 teaspoon brown sugar
½ teaspoon ground cinnamon
¼ teaspoon ground cloves

At home: combine all of the ingredients in a zip locking plastic bag or other airtight container.

In camp: add the mix to 8 ounces of hot water. Stir well before drinking.

Variation: add 1-2 teaspoons powdered hot chocolate mix to make this a mocha.

Orange Spice Coffee Mix
Makes 1/3 cup

1/3 cup instant coffee
2 tablespoons orange drink mix
½ teaspoon ground cinnamon
pinch ground cloves

At home: combine all of the ingredients in a zip locking plastic bag or other airtight container.

In camp: add the mix to hot water to taste.

Variations: add powdered milk or creamer. Add 1/3 cup dry hot chocolate mix to make this a spicy orange mocha.

Hazelnut Almond Mocha
Serves 1

1-2 packets hazelnut flavored instant coffee
2 tablespoons powdered almond milk
1 packet hot chocolate mix

At home: combine all of the ingredients in a zip locking plastic bag.

In camp: add the mix to 8 ounces hot water.

Cocktails

Everyone who knows anything about me knows that I love a boozy beverage. Every time I go to the liquor store it seems like there is yet another new product in those cute little mini bottles. I had a lot of fun using those to create creative trail cocktails for this book. These make nice treats in camp when you are sitting around swapping trail stories after dinner.

Backpacking is not the time or place to get sloppy drunk and out of control. Please drink responsibly and pack out the empties.

X-Rated Lemonade
Serves 1-2

I bring a full size bottle of this to an annual car camping trip in Colorado every year. It is always one of the first to be emptied. It may be bright pink, but even the manly men like it.

2 tablespoons lemonade drink mix
1 mini bottle X-rated Fusion

At home: package the lemonade and liquor separately.

In camp: for each serving, add 1 tablespoon to 6 ounces cold water. Stir in half of the liquor. Serve.

BeeMan Hot Toddy
Serves 1

Every year I fly down to California to attend the Annual Day Zero Pacific Crest Trail Kick Off, ADZPCTKO, or just "kick off" and every year I completely lose my voice. Blame it on the dry air or just me talking too much, but *every year* I go mute. I've tried a variety of remedies and none of them work, but this one made me very happy. My friend, BeeMan, raises bees and he gifted me with a jar of his delicious honey. For a trail friendly version I use the small packets of honey in this recipe.

1 mini bottle of whiskey or bourbon
1-2 packets honey
1 black tea bag

Add the tea bag to 8 ounces of hot water and allow to steep until the tea is as strong as you would like it. Pour in the whiskey and then stir in honey to taste.

Springer Mountain Cooler
Serves 1-2

This one is for those of us who don't like sweet cocktails.

1-2 tablespoons lemonade drink mix
1 mini bottle cucumber flavored vodka

At home: package the lemonade and vodka separately.

In camp: add the lemonade to 6-8 ounces cold water. Stir in the vodka and serve.

Green Mountain Martini
Serves 1-2

This cocktail is mossy green in color, but very tasty.

1 packet instant unsweetened iced green tea
1 mini bottle lemon flavored vodka

At home: package the tea and liquor separately.

In camp: add the green tea to 6-8 ounces cold water. Stir in the vodka and serve.

Chapter 2 - Breakfast

What kind of morning person are you? Do you like to linger over breakfast, eating gourmet trail pancakes and chatting with friends, or do you want something quick and no-cook so you can hit the trail right away?

Breakfast is "the most important meal of the day." You have to have fuel in your body if you are going to get up and get hiking.

In very cold or very wet weather you might want to plan for some easy snacks that you can eat before you get out of your sleeping bag. Choose things that are not messy, such as fruit snacks, jerky or trail bars.

The best backcountry breakfast I ever remember having was not intended to be a breakfast at all. We ran out of time and daylight to prepare dessert the night before, so we ate dessert for breakfast! Imagine eating a delicious instant cheesecake and sipping coffee while the morning sun rises at Upper Royal Basin and the surrounding peaks in the Olympic Mountains. Perfection!

Maple Nut Oatmeal
Serves 1

1 packet plain instant oatmeal
1 packet maple syrup (take out)
1/2 teaspoon ground cinnamon
1 teaspoon brown sugar
2 tablespoons slivered almonds (or other nuts)
1 teaspoon powdered milk

At home: combine all of the dry ingredients in a zip locking plastic bag. Drop the packet of syrup in the bag.

In camp: remove the syrup from the bag. Add 2/3 cup boiling water to oatmeal (or more if you like a thinner cereal.) Stir in syrup before eating.

Carrot Cake Oatmeal
Serves 1

Adjust serving size as needed. Sugar Momma and Stumbling Norwegian tested this on their PCT hike. I doubled the recipe for Norwegian. The carrots can be a little chewy, especially if they are home-dried, but they add a nice texture to the oatmeal.

1 packet plain instant oatmeal
1 1/2 tablespoons dried carrots
1 tablespoon raisins
1 tablespoon powdered milk
1 teaspoon brown sugar (or more, to taste)
1/4 teaspoon ground cinnamon
1/8 teaspoon ground nutmeg

At home: combine all of the dry ingredients in a zip locking plastic bag.

In camp: add 2/3 cup boiling water to oatmeal (or more if you like a thinner cereal.)

Apple Cinnamon Oatmeal
Serves 1

1 packet plain instant oatmeal
1 tablespoon brown sugar
3 tablespoons dried apples, chopped
1 teaspoon cinnamon
1/2 tablespoon powdered milk
pinch nutmeg

At home: combine everything in a zip locking plastic bag.

In camp: add 2/3 cup boiling water to oatmeal (or more if you like a thinner cereal.) Stir, let sit for 1 minute and eat!

Pina Colada Oatmeal
Serves 1

1 packet plain instant oatmeal
1 tablespoon coconut crème powder
1 dried pineapple ring, finely chopped
1 tablespoon macadamia nuts, finely chopped
1 teaspoon shredded coconut
1 teaspoon powdered milk
1 packet honey

At home: combine everything except the honey in a zip locking plastic bag.

In camp: add 2/3 cup boiling water to oatmeal (or more if you like a thinner cereal.) Stir, let sit for 1 minute. Stir in the honey just before eating.

Cherry Peach Couscous
Serves 1

1/3 cup couscous
1 tablespoon dried cherries, chopped
2 tablespoons dried peaches, chopped
1/8 teaspoon allspice
1 teaspoon brown sugar
1 tablespoon powdered milk

At home: combine everything in a zip locking plastic bag.

In camp: add enough hot water to cover. Stir well and let sit for 5 minutes or until the couscous is tender.

Coconut Ginger Couscous
Serves 1

This is especially good on cold mornings. The ginger gives it a little heat and is nicely chewy.

1/3 cup couscous
4 tablespoons coconut crème powder
2 tablespoons candied ginger, finely chopped
2 tablespoons powdered milk
1 tablespoon brown sugar
1/t ground ginger

At home: combine all of the ingredients in a zip locking plastic bag.

In camp: add enough hot water to cover. Stir well and let sit for 5 minutes or until the couscous is tender.

Mango Lime Coconut Rice
Serves 1

This was one of Sugar Momma's favorites on her PCT hike. Just the right amount of sweetness and tang to start your day.

1/3 cup instant rice
2 packets True Lime
1 tablespoon coconut crème powder
2 tablespoons dried mango, chopped
1/8 teaspoon allspice
1 teaspoon brown sugar
1 tablespoon powdered milk

At home: combine everything except the honey in a zip locking plastic bag. Carry that separately.

In camp: add enough water to cover. Let stand until rice is tender.

Cran-Orange Breakfast Bulgur
Serves 1

1/4 cup bulgur
2 tablespoon dried cranberries
2 packets True Orange
1 tablespoon powdered milk
2 teaspoon brown sugar
1/4 teaspoon cinnamon

At home: combine everything in a zip locking plastic bag.

In camp: add about 1/2 cup water (enough to cover). Stir and let stand for 5 minutes or until bulgur is tender.

Peanut Butter Banana Pancakes
Serves 2

Make sure that the peanut butter is mixed into the batter very well. It has a tendency to burn if left in large clumps.

1 cup just-add-water pancake mix
2 tablespoons peanut butter (or 1 1.15 ounce packet)
¼ cup freeze dried bananas, crushed
¼ teaspoon ground cinnamon
vegetable oil

At home: combine all of the dry ingredients in a zip locking plastic bag. Carry the peanut butter and oil separately.

In camp: add ¾ cup water to the bag. Squish well to combine, then add the peanut butter. Squish until there are no more large lumps of peanut butter in the bag. Heat a little oil in your pan. Snip off one end of the plastic bag and pour out enough batter to make 3 inch pancakes. When bubbles form on the top, flip. Serve hot.

Variation: add 1 tablespoon mini chocolate chips to the dry ingredients.

Double Almond Pancakes
Serves 2-3

Powdered almond milk can be found in the bulk bins of some grocery stores, at Asian markets and online. Watch these carefully because the high sugar content of the almond milk causes them to brown very quickly.

1 cup just-add-water pancake mix
3 tablespoons powdered almond milk
3 tablespoons ground almonds
1 teaspoon ground cinnamon
freshly picked huckleberries (optional)
vegetable oil

At home: combine all of the dry ingredients in a zip locking plastic bag.

In camp: add about 2/3 cup water to the bag. Squish well to combine. Heat a little oil in your pan. Snip off one end of the plastic bag and pour out enough batter to make 3 inch pancakes. Sprinkle huckleberries on top. When bubbles form on the top, flip. Serve hot.

Pretty in Pink
Serves 1

This is a great portable breakfast.

1 large flour tortilla
1 1 ounce package strawberry cream cheese
1/4 cup freeze dried strawberries (bananas would be good too -
or both!)

At home: wrap the tortilla in foil. Place the strawberries in zip
locking plastic bag.

In camp: spread the tortilla with the cream cheese. Top with the
strawberries. Roll and eat.

Hoosierdaddy's Grits
Serves 1 manly man

Make sure you buy *instant* grits or this recipe will not work.

3 packets instant grits
2 tablespoons shelf stable bacon bits (or more to taste)
1 packet butter

At home: combine everything in a zip locking plastic bag.

In camp: add hot water slowly to the bag. Your grits should not
be soupy. Place in a cozy and let stand for 6-8 minutes. Stir well
before serving.

Variations: add coconut crème powder, onion flakes or red
pepper flakes to taste.

Veggie Tofu Scramble
Serves 1-2

Heat a little extra water while making your coffee in the morning and you will be one step ahead for this recipe. Look for tofu in shelf stable tetra packs.

8 ounces firm or extra firm tofu
½ cup dried mixed vegetables
1 teaspoon vegetable bouillon
Olive oil
Parmesan cheese to taste

At home: place the vegetables and bouillon in a zip locking freezer bag. Carry the other ingredients separately.

In camp: bring about half a cup of water to boil. Add to the vegetables. Seal the bag and set aside in a cozy to keep warm.

Heat a couple of tablespoons of oil in your pan. If the tofu is not in a tetra pack, drain it as well as possible. Break up the tofu slightly while it is still in the container. Add to the hot oil in the pan, mashing with a fork. Cook until heated through and starting to brown, about 5 minutes.

Add the rehydrated vegetables to the pan and stir well to combine. Heat through if needed. Serve topped with Parmesan cheese.

Potato Egg Scramble
Serves 1-2

I know a recipe is a keeper when my dear hubby says he likes it. He said it only needed a little salt and pepper and skipped the hot/mild sauce.

For a portable breakfast, try wrapping this recipe in a tortilla.

1 cup dried potato shreds
2 fresh eggs
2 tablespoons mixed vegetables
½ teaspoon oregano
2 slices cheese
oil for frying
salt and pepper to taste
2 packets hot/mild sauce (or more to taste)

At home: combine the potato shreds, mixed vegetables and oregano in a zip locking freezer bag. Carefully package the eggs for the trail.

In camp: add just enough water to cover the potatoes. Let stand for 5 minutes. Crack the eggs into the bag, seal and squish until thoroughly combined. The mixture will be very wet.

Heat a pan over moderate heat and coat lightly with oil. Pour the contents of the bag into the pan and scramble until cooked through, about 5 minutes. Serve topped with cheese and hot/mild sauce.

McMountain Breakfast Sandwich
Serves 1

Kids like this breakfast, especially if they get to help with the cooking.

1 English muffin or sandwich thin, split
1 boiled egg
2 slices cheese
1-2 packets butter

At home: wrap the English muffin in foil. Carry all of the other ingredients separately.

In camp: unwrap the English muffin, reserving the foil. Spread each side with butter. Peel and slice the egg. Layer a slice of cheese, then egg, and then the second slice of cheese on one side of the English muffin. Cover with the second side and wrap in foil.

Place in a pan over moderate heat and fry until heated through and cheese is melted, about 5 minutes. Make sure to turn the sandwich often to prevent burning. Unwrap the foil and eat hot.

Chapter 3 - Lunches

It is really hard to come up with new ideas for trail lunches. I tend to return to the same tried and true things over and over again. Some of my favorite lunches are hard boiled eggs, salami with cheese and crackers, hummus and pita chips and/or carrots. Often I do not take a lunch break at all and just snack my way through the day; sort of a continual lunch fest. Lunch does not have to be a once a day event. A friend of mine often slips hard candies into my pockets and reminds me that they are good for a quick boost of instant energy.

Even favorite foods can get tedious if you are eating the same things day after day. I have made an effort to either spice up the same boring meals we all know, or try new combinations of ingredients. The idea is to make things more interesting, not more difficult.

It seems like I find new trail friendly products or new flavors of existing products every day. The same old crackers with a new type of cheese spread may just be the thing to perk up your mid day meal.

Lunch does not have to be about trail bars and dried fruit. My friend, Hoosierdaddy, swears by my wrap recipes. These can be toted along with you as you hike, negating the need for long lunch breaks, unless you want one. There are a myriad of different ways of making them. Try the various flavors of tortilla now on the market for a little more variety in your lunches. I have seen spinach, sun dried tomato, pumpernickle, rye and various herb-flavored tortillas. Gluten free varieties are also becoming easier to find.

Don't limit yourself to the recipes in this book. Use your imagination and find your own favorite combinations. Some ideas for the "glue" part of a wrap include hummus, instant black beans, instant refried beans, cream cheese (in various flavors), peanut or other nut butters, spreadable cheese wedges and mashed avocados. Try different sauces or salad dressings too. Barbeque sauce and ranch dressing are great on tortillas with some vegetables or cheese.

On the other hand, lunch can also be a good time to take an extended break at a beautiful lake or other scenic spot. Eat your largest meal of the day while taking in the scenery. Take your boots off and soak your feet while enjoying a leisurely meal. You will be rested and able to hit the trail completely refreshed. This also allows you more freedom later in the day because you will not necessarily need a campsite that has access to water. You have done your cooking at lunchtime, so dinner can be simple.

Another alternative for lunch is to eat a no-cook dinner or breakfast. Many of the lunch recipes can also be used for dinner.

On fall and winter trips, I will often cook a quick lunch. Soup and couscous dishes are great for warming you up in the middle of a cold day. My daughter loves quesadillas, which are fairly fast to put together on the trail.

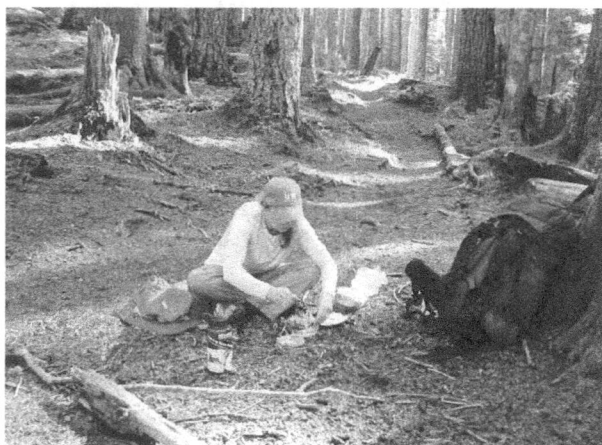

Esmeralda Wrap
Serves 1

This is what I am about to eat on the cover of book #1.

1 large flour tortilla
4 strips shelf stable bacon slices
1 ounce packet shelf stable cream cheese
1 fresh avocado
2 sun dried tomatoes

At home: wrap the tortilla in foil. Cut the sun dried tomatoes in tiny pieces and put in a small zip locking bag. Carry the bacon and cream cheese separately.

In camp: spread the tortilla with cream cheese. Top with all of the bacon. Cut the avocado in half and scoop out the flesh. Top the bacon with half of the avocado (eat the other half!). Sprinkle with sun dried tomatoes. Roll and eat!

Mount Daniel Wrap
Serves 1

This is one of my favorite go-to lunches. It is wicked easy and delicious!

1 large flour tortilla
1/3 cup instant black or refried beans
1-2 taco or hot sauce packets
2 baby bell cheese wheels

At home: put the beans in a snack sized baggie. Carry everything else seperately.

In camp: add water to the bean baggie. Seal and squish. Let stand for 5 minutes or until rehydrated. Cut a corner off the bag and squish out onto a tortilla (like you are piping frosting!) Top with the hot sauce. Unwrap the cheese, cut in half and top the beans with them. Roll and eat.

Seattle Wrap
Serves 1

I would assemble this at home. You make it on the trail, but it may be a little fussy.

1 large flour tortilla
1 ounce package shelf stable cream cheese
¼ teaspoon wasabi powder
1 foil pouch salmon
fresh spinach or arugula to taste

Spread the cream cheese evenly on the tortilla. Sprinkle with wasabi powder. Spoon the salmon over the top. Add spinach or arugula and roll like a burrito.

Cali Wrap
Serves 1

This is another assemble at home lunch.

1 large tortilla
1-2 wedges of spreadable blue cheese
2 tablespoons soft sun dried tomatoes, chopped
1 cup fresh spinach
4 slices deli turkey

Spread the blue cheese evenly on the tortilla. Lay the turkey slices flat over the top. Sprinkle with sun dried tomatoes and spinach. Roll like a burrito.

Athenos Wrap
Serves 1

On longer trips wait until you get to camp to slice the vegetables. The larger the pieces of vegetables, the longer they will last in your backpack.

1 large tortilla
2 tablespoons instant hummus powder
1 tablespoon sliced red onion
¼ cucumber, thinly sliced

At home: wrap the tortilla in foil. Place the hummus in a small zip locking plastic bag or other airtight container. Place the onion in another bag and the cucumber in a third.

In camp: add enough water to the hummus to make a smooth, spreadable paste. Spread the hummus evenly on the tortilla and then sprinkle with the onions. Top with the cucumber and then roll like a burrito.

Thai Me Up Wrap
Serves 1

The cabbage in this recipe is optional, but it gives the wrap a nice crunch.

1 large tortilla
¼ cup shredded cabbage (optional)
¼ cup instant rice
1 tablespoon peanut sauce mix powder
1 tablespoon coconut crème powder
1 tablespoon dried chicken
1 teaspoon dried bell pepper

At home: wrap the tortilla in foil. Package all of the dry ingredients separately in a zip locking plastic bag. If you are using the cabbage, place that in a second bag.

In camp: about 15-20 minutes before you plan to eat, add enough water to cover the rice mixture. Stir well to combine and let stand. When the rice is tender, stir again and spread on the tortilla. Add the cabbage and roll like a burrito.

Southern Wrap
Serves 1

1 large tortilla
1 ounce packet barbecue sauce
¼ cup instant rice
¼ cup fresh spinach or shredded cabbage
3 tablespoons dried chicken

At home: wrap the tortilla in foil. Package the dry ingredients separately in a zip locking plastic bag. Place the spinach or cabbage in a second bag

In camp: about 15-20 minutes before you plan to eat, add enough water to cover the rice and chicken. Stir well to combine and let stand. When the rice is tender, spread the barbecue sauce on the tortilla and top with the rice. Add the spinach or cabbage and roll like a burrito.

Heybrook Bagel
Serves 1

Make this at home before your hike.

1 bagel
1 ounce cream cheese
1 teaspoon honey
1 teaspoon Dijon mustard
2 tablespoons bacon bits
2 slices Swiss cheese

Slice the bagel in half. Spread one half with the Dijon mustard, then the honey. Top this with bacon bits. Spread the other half with cream cheese. Top with the Swiss cheese. Close sandwich and wrap tightly in foil or plastic wrap for the trail.

White Blaze Salmon Dip
Serves 1-2

1 foil pouch salmon
2 packages shelf stable cream cheese
2 packets True Lemon (or more to taste)
1 teaspoon dried tarragon
1 teaspoon dried shallots or onion flakes
crackers, tortillas or bread for serving

At home: combine the True Lemon, tarragon and shallots in a zip locking bag. Carry the salmon and cream cheese in a second bag (with your crackers). It is less messy this way.

In camp: add the salmon and cream cheese to the bag with the herbs. Close the bag and squish well until completely combined. Either dip or spoon onto crackers, tortilla or bread.

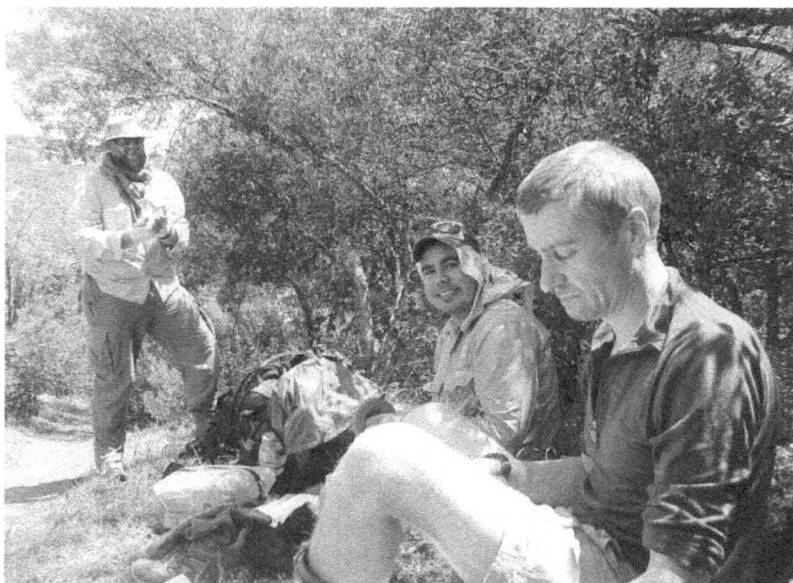

Lentil Tapenade
Serves 1

Serve with crackers and cheese. Aged white cheddar is especially delicious with this spread.

¼ cup cooked and dehydrated lentils
1 tablespoon sun dried tomatoes, finely chopped
1 teaspoon dried parsley
½ teaspoon vegetable or chicken bouillon
¼ teaspoon garlic powder
1 packet True Lemon
salt, pepper and olive oil to taste

At home: combine all of the ingredients in a zip locking plastic bag.

In camp: add just enough water to cover. Stir well. When the lentils are rehydrated stir again before serving.

Ginger Curry Hummus
Serves 1-2

Serve with carrot sticks. The sweetness of the carrots pairs beautifully with the spice of the curry. I had fun feeding this to a bunch of hungry thru hikers at Urich Cabin.

For a more substantial lunch, spread this on a tortilla and top with shredded cabbage and carrots.

½ cup instant hummus powder
1 tablespoon curry powder
1 teaspoon ground ginger
Olive oil to taste (optional)

At home: combine the hummus, curry powder and ginger in a zip locking plastic bag.

In camp: add enough water to make a dip like consistency, stirring well. Serve on vegetables, pita, tortillas or crackers.

Mexicalli Hummus
Serves 1-2

This makes more than you would think. Stir well before serving or you end up with lumps of spice. Serve on a corn tortilla with avocado or with corn chips. The saltiness of the chips pairs nicely with the spice and creaminess of the beans.

½ cup instant refried beans
1 teaspoon dried cilantro
1 teaspoon chili powder
1 packet True Lemon
2 packets True Lime
½ teaspoon ground cumin
¼ teaspoon garlic powder
pinch cayenne (or more to taste)

At home: combine all of the ingredients in a zip locking plastic bag.

In camp: add enough water to make a dip or spread like consistency, stirring well. Serve as a dip with chips or as a spread on tortillas.

Chapter 4 - Snacks and Trail Mixes

Morning Gorp
Makes 1 1/2 cups

This is a great portable breakfast!

¼ cup chocolate covered coffee beans
¼ cup dried cranberries or cherries
¼ cup candied walnuts or almonds
¼ cup yogurt covered raisins
½ cup granola clusters

Combine everything in a zip locking plastic bag. Munch by the handfuls.

ET's Mix
Makes about 2 cups

I have to give my husband credit for this one. It is really his creation. If you look very closely at the cover of book #1, this mix is featured.

2 single serving bags Reese's Pieces
1 cup dry roasted peanuts
1/2 cup raisins

Combine everything in a zip locking plastic bag. Munch by the handfuls.

Fancy Gorp
Makes 1 cup

1/2 cup honey roasted peanuts
1/4 cup yogurt covered raisins
1/4 cup chocolate covered raisins

Combine everything in a zip locking plastic bag. Munch by the handfuls.

Berry Blend Gorp
Makes 2 cups

1/3 cup each dried blueberries, golden raisins and dried cranberries
1 cup dry roasted peanuts

Combine everything in a zip locking plastic bag. Munch by the handfuls.

Strawberry Fields Forever
Makes 1 ¾ cups

1 cup frosted Strawberry Mini Wheats cereal
¼ cup freeze dried strawberries
¼ cup chocolate chips
¼ cup yogurt covered cranberries (or raisins)

Combine everything in a zip locking plastic bag. Munch by the handfuls.

Sunshine on the Ridge Mix
Makes 1 ¼ cups

¼ cup pumpkin seeds
¼ cup golden raisins
¼ cup dried mangos, diced
¼ cup sunflower seeds
¼ cup Marcona almonds or slivered almonds

Combine everything in a zip locking plastic bag. Munch by the handfuls.

Toddler Mix
Makes 1 cup

1/3 cup plain teddy grahams
1/3 cup dried cranberries
1/3 cup mini M&Ms

Combine everything in a zip locking plastic bag. Munch by the handfuls.

Pickle Gulch Apricot Bites
Make about 4 dozen

16 ounces of dried apricots
7 ounce tube of almond paste
12 ounce bag of semi sweet chocolate chips

Stuff each apricot with about ½ teaspoon of almond paste. Press edges together to seal as well as possible. Repeat until all of the apricots are stuffed.

Melt the chocolate in the microwave. Dip each apricot in melted chocolate and set on waxed or parchment paper to set. Store in an airtight container or refrigerate.

Variations: sprinkle with ground almonds, chopped pistachios, candied orange zest or cocoa powder while chocolate is still wet.

Five Spice Peanuts
Makes 2 cups

These are both sweet and spicy with a nice crunch. Surprisingly enough, both the kidling and the hubby love them!

2 cups roasted, unsalted peanuts
3 tablespoons butter
¼ cup brown sugar
1 tablespoon light corn syrup
½ teaspoon five-spice powder
¼ teaspoon salt

Line a baking sheet with foil or parchment paper, or spray with cooking spray.

In a small saucepan, melt the butter, sugar and corn syrup over medium heat to dissolve the sugar. Stir in the five-spice powder and bring to a boil; let boil for several minutes without stirring; when it reaches the "soft ball" stage (238*F) remove from the heat and stir in the peanuts.

Spread the peanuts out on the baking sheet; let stand until they have cooled completely and then break into pieces. Store in an airtight container.

Ginger Peanuts
Makes 2 cups

This simple mix has it all; salty, sweet and spicy. It is especially good on snowshoeing trips.

1 cup Spanish peanuts
1 cup candied ginger, cut in tiny pieces

At home: combine both ingredients

In camp: eat by the handfuls.

Splash's Fruit Bars

Splash was nice enough to allow me to use her recipe for these trail bars. They are a homemade version of another popular bar. She uses cranberries and golden raisins for the mixed fruit, but the possibilities here are endless.

10 ounces pitted dates
1 cup dried plums
2 cups slivered almonds
1 teaspoon almond extract
1/2 teaspoon cinnamon
1/4 cup creamy peanut butter
5 ounces dried mixed fruits

Mix about 2 minutes in food processor until a paste forms.

Press into a parchment lined 8x8 pan. Chill overnight or freeze for 30 minutes before slicing into bars.

To keep the bars from being overly sticky, coat them in a mixture of ground pecans and cocoa powder, ground pistachios, or ground almonds

Wrap in wax paper for the trail.

Sesame Peanut Bites
Makes about 2 dozen

If you spray your measuring cups with cooking spray before measuring the honey and peanut butter, clean up will be much easier.

1 cup powdered milk
2/3 cup finely chopped peanuts
1/3 cup sesame seeds
½ cup honey
½ cup peanut butter
½ cup shredded unsweetened coconut
cooking spray

In a saucepan, melt honey and peanut butter together. Remove from heat and add powdered milk, coconut, sesame seeds and peanuts. Stir until well combined.

Pat into a greased 8 by 8 inch baking pan. Refrigerate until set and then cut into 1 inch cubes. Wrap in foil or plastic wrap. Store in the refrigerator or freezer until your hike.

Latte Bars

3 eggs
1 1/2 cups sugar
2 tsp vanilla
1/4 cup butter, melted
2 cups all-purpose flour
1/2 tsp salt
1/4 cup instant coffee crystals
1/4 cup milk or heavy cream
1 cup pecans, chopped
1/2 cup mini chocolate chips

At home: Preheat oven to 325° F. Lightly grease a 13 x 9 inch pan. Beat the eggs in a mixing bowl until light and fluffy.

Add the sugar, vanilla and butter, beating to combine. Stir in the flour and salt. Set aside 1 1/2 cups of batter. Stir the coffee crystals and cream and add to the remaining batter. Spread the coffee batter into the prepared pan.

Add chocolate chips to the reserved batter and spoon over the coffee batter. Run a knife through the two batters to marble them. Sprinkle the pecans over the top.

Bake 20-25 minutes or until the center is firm and set. Cool before cutting into bars. Wrap tightly in plastic wrap or foil. Store in the freezer.

In camp: Unwrap and enjoy!

Chapter 5 - Salads

When I am in the backcountry, one of the things I crave most is a big, green crunchy salad. I am a big believer in feeding your body what it is craving. Carrot sticks, apple wedges, snap and snow peas all travel well. Bring along a small packet of take-out salad dressing and you'll be having delicious salads in camp in no time. Dried vegetables added to meals up the nutritional value without a lot of extra weight.

Fresh food on hard trips is not only delicious, it can be mentally satisfying. Imagine pulling something fresh, with color and texture, out of your food bag after days of nothing but carbs and other mush.

One very memorable trip, my friends and I were hiking into the Upper Enchantments in the Alpine Lakes Wilderness in the fall. Of course we started talking about food and one of my friends, Fireball, was giving me a bad time for the whole apple I had in my pack. After we climbed over Asgaard Pass (2200 feet of elevation gain in ¾ of a mile) we stopped for lunch. I sat down and started to eat my nice crunchy, juicy red apple. Fireball looked at his bagel and cheese sandwich, then at me, then back at his sandwich before he finally asked for a bite of the apple. I had a good laugh at his expense, but I did give him a bite. That apple tasted better than any other apple I have ever eaten. I earned it!

It's in the Bag Trail Salad
Serves 1-2

There are ready-to-eat bagged salad kits that already contain things like grilled chicken, dried cranberries, croutons, nuts and salad dressing. Just buy one of these and you are set to go!

1 bag ready-made salad mix
other trail friendly vegetables of your choice
1-2 packets of your favorite salad dressing

Unstuffed Tomato Salad
Serves 1

Add more water than you think you will need for this salad. It really sucks up the water.

This can also be served on a pita or in a tortilla. It is especially nice on sun-dried tomato flavored tortillas with a little fresh spinach added.

½ cup instant tabbouleh mix
3 tablespoons dried tomatoes
½ teaspoon onion flakes
olive oil to taste

At home: combine all of the dry ingredients in a zip locking plastic bag.

In camp: add enough water to cover. Stir well and let stand until the salad is tender and the tomatoes are rehydrated.

Dilly Tuna Salad
Serves 1

This can be served on crackers, bread or by itself.

1 foil pouch tuna
2 tablespoons dried vegetables
1 teaspoon dried dill
1 packet True Lemon
1/2 teaspoon vegetable bouillon
2 packets mayo

At home: combine the vegetables, dill, True Lemon and bouillon in a zip locking plastic bag. Carry the other ingredients separately.

In camp: add just enough water to the vegetables to cover. Let stand for 5 minutes, or until rehydrated. Add the tuna and mayo. Stir well and enjoy.

White Bean and Fennel Salad
Serves 1

1/4 fresh fennel bulb
1 foil pouch tuna
1/3 cup (cooked) dried white beans
1 tablespoon dried parsley
1 packet True Lemon (or more, to taste)
1/4 teaspoon dried oregano
olive oil to taste
salt and pepper to taste

At home: combine all of the dried ingredients in a zip locking plastic bag. Place the fennel and tuna in a second bag. Carry the olive oil in a screw top container.

In camp: add enough water to the dry ingredients to cover the beans. Allow to rehydrate. Meanwhile, dice the fennel (the smaller, the better). Stir the fennel and tuna into the bean mixture. Season with salt, pepper and olive oil to taste.

American River Sunshine Salad
Serves 1

If you use couscous instead of quinoa, no dehydrator is needed. Red wine vinegar may be used in place of the champagne vinegar.

1/3 cup (cooked and dried) quinoa
3 packets True Orange
2 tablespoons golden raisins
1 teaspoon dried parsley
1/2 teaspoon dried shallots
1/2 teaspoon vegetable bouillon
1/4 teaspoon ground cumin
1 teaspoon champagne vinegar
1 tablespoon olive oil

At home: combine all of the ingredients except the oil and vinegar in a zip locking plastic bag. Combine the oil and vinegar in a screw top container.

In camp: add just enough water to cover. Stir well and allow to rehydrate. Add the oil and vinegar (to taste) just before serving.

Obi's Salad
Serves 1

1/3 cup (cooked) dried chickpeas
2 tablespoons dried peas
1 foil pouch salmon
11 ounce package balsamic salad dressing

At home: combine the chickpeas and peas in a zip locking plastic bag. Place the salad dressing and salmon in the bag for storage.

In camp: remove the salad dressing and salmon. Add just enough water to cover and allow the chickpeas and peas to rehydrate (about 10 minutes). Stir in the salmon, breaking up any large chunks. Stir in the salad dressing and eat.

Lentil Bulgur Salad

This is intended to be a first night meal. Omit the feta and it can be eaten on any night of your journey.

1/4 cup (cooked and dehydrated) lentils
1/4 cup bulgur
2 tablespoons dried tomatoes
1/2 tablespoon onion flakes
1 teaspoon dried parsley
1 packet True Lemon
2 tablespoons feta cheese (optional)

At home: combine all of the ingredients except the feta in a zip locking plastic bag. Carry the feta in a second bag.

In camp: Add 1/2 to 3/4 cup hot water to the lentils and bulgur. Stir to combine and allow to rehydrate before topping with the feta cheese.

Chicken Curry Quinoa Salad
Serves 1

This has a nice little kick from the curry powder. Remember to stir well before eating! It can be served hot or cold.

1/3 cup cooked and dehydrated quinoa
1/4 cup freeze dried corn
3 tablespoons dehydrated chicken
2 tablespoons dried mixed vegetables
1 teaspoon curry powder
1 teaspoon onion flakes
1 teaspoon chicken or vegetable bullion
1/2 teaspoon dried cilantro
1/4 teaspoon garlic powder

At home: combine all of the ingredients in a zip locking plastic bag.

In camp: add enough hot or cold water to cover (about 1 cup). Allow to rehydrate. Stir well before eating.

Black Bean and Corn Salad
Serves 1

1/3 cup instant corn chowder (from bulk bins)
1/3 cup dried black beans
2 tablespoons dried bell peppers
1 tablespoon onion flakes
1 tablespoon dried cilantro
½ teaspoon ground cumin
1 packet balsamic salad dressing

At home: combine all of the dry ingredients in a zip locking bag.

In camp: add just enough water to cover. Set aside for 5-10 minutes and allow to rehydrate. Add dressing to taste. Stir well and enjoy.

Chapter 6 - Soups

Soups can warm you up, rehydrate you and take almost no time in camp to prepare. Sometimes, upon arriving at camp, I just do not have an appetite for dinner. This is usually because I am slightly dehydrated. If I sip a cup of instant soup, my appetite usually returns and I am able to cook and eat a delicious dinner.

Sometimes you roll into camp and it is too early for dinner, but you want a little something. Soup might just be the thing. Sip on a cup of Instant Chicken Curry Soup while doing camp chores or just taking in the scenery. Sipping on some soup won't fill you up, but it will help to rehydrate you and in some cases replace important electrolytes and nutrients.

It is especially nice to have soups on cold weather trips. Sitting around camp in the cold is a sure way to get chilled. Having a hot soup or beverage will help warm you from the inside out.

Miso Mushroom Soup
Serves 1-2
2 ounces

Warner Springs Monty calls this a "thru hiker's dream dinner."
Feel free to use whatever kind of mushrooms you like.

1 0.94 ounce package instant miso soup
1 tablespoon dried mixed vegetables
4 tablespoons dried shiitake mushrooms, broken up
1 tablespoon dried oyster mushrooms
1 tablespoon dried wood ear mushrooms

At home: package the mushrooms and vegetables in a zip
locking plastic bag. Carry the miso soup mix separately.

In camp: bring 2-3 cups of water to a boil. Add to mushrooms.
Allow the mushrooms to rehydrate before adding the soup mix.

Tomato Basil Lentil Soup
Serves 1

Dried lentils can be purchased online or made at home in the dehydrator. Check the bulk bins of herbs and spices at your grocery store for tomato powder. It is also available online.

1/4 cup (cooked) dried lentils
1 tablespoon dried tomatoes
1 tablespoon tomato powder
1 teaspoon chicken or vegetable bouillon
2 teaspoons dried carrots
1/2 teaspoon dried basil
1 teaspoon onion flakes
1/4 teaspoon onion powder
1/2 teaspoon dried oregano
1/2 teaspoon dried parsley
salt and pepper to taste

At home: combine all of the ingredients in a zip locking plastic bag.

In camp: add enough hot water to cover. Allow to rehydrate. Add more water to reach desired consistency.

Split Pea and Bacon Soup
Serves 1-2

This soup is a result of a crazy food challenge. Someone told me I couldn't make a split pea and bacon soup for the trail. I set out to prove them wrong... And I did!

1/3 cup green split peas (either soup mix or cooked and dried)
2 tablespoons shelf stable bacon
1 tablespoon dried carrots
1 tablespoon dried potato shreds
1 teaspoon onion flakes
1 teaspoon dried celery (or 1/4 teaspoon celery seeds)
1 teaspoon chicken bouillon
1/2 teaspoon dried parsley

At home: combine everything in a zip locking plastic bag.

In camp: add more than enough water to cover. Stir well and then place in a cozy. Let stand 5 minutes. Add more water if needed.

Oyster Veggie Leek Stew
Serves 2

3.75 ounce can smoked oysters
1.8 ounce package leek soup mix
2 tablespoons dried mixed vegetables
½ cup dried potato slices, broken up
½ cup powdered milk
Salt and pepper to taste

At home: combine the powdered milk, soup mix and vegetables in a zip locking plastic bag. Carry the oysters separately.

In camp: bring about 3 cups of water to a boil. Add the soup mix, stirring, to break up any lumps. When the vegetables are rehydrated, add the oysters and their juice and simmer until heated through. Season with salt and pepper to taste.

Backpacker's Quinoa Soup with Avocado and Corn
Serves 1

Sarbar had sent me a great original recipe for this soup, which I promptly converted to be trail friendly. If you swap out the quinoa for couscous, no dehydrator is required.

1/4 cup (cooked and dehydrated) quinoa
2 tablespoons freeze dried corn
2 tablespoons dried mixed vegetables
1 tablespoon tomato powder
1 1/2 teaspoons vegetable bouillon
1 teaspoon dried cilantro
1 packet True Lime
1 fresh avocado
salt and pepper to taste

At home: combine all of the dry ingredients in a zip locking plastic bag. Carry the avocado separately.

In camp: bring about 1 1/2 cups water to a boil. Add the dry ingredients. Stir and allow to rehydrate. Dice the avocado and stir it into the soup. Season to taste with salt and pepper.

Instant Chicken Curry Soup
Serves 1

The flavor for this soup depends heavily on your bouillon and curry powders. Use good ones! The spicier the curry, the more kick your soup will have. This is a great treat on winter nights in the back country. It is easily made into a vegetarian soup by using chicken flavored textured vegetable protein.

1 teaspoon chicken bouillon powder
1 teaspoon curry powder
2 tablespoons instant rice or couscous
2-3 tablespoons dried chicken (or a 3 ounce can)
3 tablespoons dried mixed vegetables
¼ teaspoon ground ginger

At home: combine everything in a zip locking plastic bag.

In camp: add more than enough water to cover. Stir well and then place in a cozy. Let stand 5 minutes. Add more water if needed.

Herbed Vegetable Broth
Serves 1

This is great to sip on while the rest of your dinner is cooking. The amount of salt you add will depend on the brand of vegetable bouillon you chose. Some are very high in sodium.

2 tablespoons dried mushrooms, broken as small as possible
1 tablespoon vegetable bouillon
1 tablespoon Italian seasoning blend
1 tablespoon sun dried tomatoes, finely chopped
salt and pepper to taste

At home: combine all of the ingredients in a zip locking plastic bag.

In camp: add the dried mix to 1 cup of hot water. Let the mushrooms rehydrate before eating.

Black White and Red Chili
Serves 1

¼ cup dried black beans (refried or soup mix)
¼ cup dried white beans (soup mix)
2 tablespoons dried tomatoes
1 tablespoon dried bell pepper
1 tablespoon chili powder
1 tablespoon dried cilantro
½ teaspoon onion flakes
½ teaspoon ground cumin
¼ teaspoon dried oregano
¼ teaspoon garlic powder
salt, pepper, olive oil to taste

At home: combine everything in a zip locking plastic bag.

In camp: add more than enough water to cover. Stir well and then place in a cozy. Let stand 5 minutes. Add more water if needed.

Black Bean and Sweet Potato Chili
Serves 1

This is not sweet, like most of us associate sweet potatoes to be. It has more of a savory, bean flavor. Freeze dried sweet potatoes work better than home dried ones in this dish, based on final texture alone.

½ cup dried sweet potatoes
¼ cup dried black beans
¼ cup textured vegetable protein
2 tablespoons dried tomatoes
1 tablespoon vegetable bouillon powder
1 teaspoon dried onion flakes
1 teaspoon ground cumin
1 teaspoon ground ginger
½ teaspoon garlic powder

At home: combine all of the ingredients in a zip locking plastic bag.

In camp: add enough hot water to cover. Place in a cozy and let sit for 5-10 minutes. Stir well before eating.

Vegetarian White Bean Chili
Serves 1

1/3 cup cooked and dehydrated white beans
2 tablespoons textured vegetable protein
2 tablespoons onion flakes
1 tablespoon dried bell peppers
2 teaspoons vegetable bouillon
1 teaspoon garlic powder
1 teaspoon ground cumin
salt and pepper

At home: combine all of the ingredients in a zip locking plastic bag.

In camp: add enough hot water to cover. Stir well. Place in a cozy and let stand for 5-10 minutes.

Asian Mushroom Soup

Serves 1
2 ounces (without soy sauce packets)

¼ cup dried shiitake mushrooms
2 tablespoons dried cloud ear mushrooms
2 tablespoons vegetable or mushroom bouillon
1 tablespoon dried button or cremini mushrooms
1 teaspoon onion flakes
½ teaspoon garlic powder
2 packets soy sauce
salt and pepper to taste

At home: combine all of the dry ingredients in a zip locking plastic bag. Carry the soy sauce packets separately.

In camp: add the soup mix to about 8 ounces hot water. Stir well to combine and then add the soy sauce.

Chapter 7 – Ramen

Chicken Ramen Soup
Serves 1

3 ounce package chicken or mushroom flavor ramen noodles
3 ounce can chicken
1 tablespoon dried corn
2 tablespoons dried shiitake mushrooms, broken up
1 tablespoon dried peas
1 packet soy sauce (or to taste)
1/2 to 1 teaspoon sesame oil, to taste
pinch red pepper flakes

At home: combine the corn, mushrooms, peas and red pepper flakes in a zip locking plastic bag. Carry the sesame oil in a screw top container.

In camp: bring 1 1/2 cups water to a boil. Break up the ramen noodles and add them, the seasoning packet and vegetables to the pan. When the noodles are almost done, add the chicken and its liquid.

Note: this is a thick soup; if you want it more "soupy" add more water.

Lemon Dill Tuna Ramen
Serves 1

3 ounce packet ramen noodles (any flavor)
2 packets (or 2 tablespoons) lemon juice
1 tablespoon dried dill
1 tablespoon dried mixed vegetables
1 foil pouch tuna
1 teaspoon vegetable or chicken bouillon
black pepper to taste

At home: discard ramen seasoning packet. Combine all of the remaining ingredients in a zip locking plastic bag. Carry the tuna separately.

In camp: bring 1 1/2 cups water to a boil. Break up the ramen noodles (if not already crushed) and add them to the pan. Simmer until the noodles and vegetables are soft. Stir in tuna just before serving.

Coconut Curry Chicken Ramen
Serves 1

3 ounce packet original or chicken ramen noodles
3 tablespoons dried mixed vegetables
2 tablespoons dried chicken (or 3 ounce can)
2 tablespoons coconut crème powder
1 tablespoon curry powder (or more to taste)

At home: Combine all of the ingredients in a zip locking plastic bag.

In camp: bring 1 1/2 cups water to a boil. Break up the ramen noodles (if not already crushed) and add everything to the pan. Simmer until the noodles and vegetables are soft.

Beef Stroganoff Ramen
Serves 1

Trashy hiker food at its best. Lightweight and heavy on the calories.

3 ounce package beef flavor ramen noodles
3 tablespoons freeze dried beef (or dried hamburger)
2 tablespoons dried mushrooms
1 tablespoon dried peas
1 ounce package shelf stable cream cheese

At home: Combine all of the ingredients except the cream cheese in a zip locking plastic bag.

In camp: bring 1 1/2 cups water to a boil. Break up the ramen noodles (if not already crushed) and add them to the pan along with the peas and beef. Simmer until the noodles and vegetables are soft. Stir in the cream cheese just before serving.

Bacon Mushroom Ramen
Serves 1

3 ounce package beef flavor ramen noodles
3 tablespoons shelf stable bacon
2 tablespoons dried mushrooms
1 tablespoon dried peas
1 boiled egg

At home: Combine all of the ingredients except the egg in a zip locking plastic bag.

In camp: bring 1 1/2 cups water to a boil. Break up the ramen noodles (if not already crushed) and add them to the pan along with the peas and bacon. Simmer until the noodles and vegetables are soft. Peel the boiled egg and cut into wedges. Add to the noodles before serving.

Chapter 8 - Breads and Sides

All of the mashed potato recipes use the just-add-water instant potatoes in small pouches, in various flavors. Each pouch is enough to make one recipe.

Many of the potato recipes originate from the "Tater Tuesday" series on the One Pan Wonders blog, where I feature a new potato recipe or product every Tuesday.

Some of the breads, like the Cinnamon Raisin Bannock, also make wonderful breakfasts. Serve with a cup of your favorite morning beverage and enjoy.

Chili Cheese Mashed Potatoes
Serves 1-2

This would also be good in a wrap with some black beans and salsa.

1 cup butter flavor instant mashed potatoes
2 teaspoons chili powder
4 tablespoons cheese powder

At home: combine all of the ingredients in a zip locking plastic bag.

In camp: add about 2 cups of hot water. Stir well and enjoy.

Cheesy Black Bean Mashed Potatoes
Serves 1-2

1 cup 4 cheese flavor instant mashed potatoes
4 tablespoons cheese powder
¼ cup instant black beans

At home: combine all of the ingredients in a zip locking plastic bag.

In camp: add 2 cups of hot water. Stir well before serving.

Lemon Paprika Mashed Potatoes
Serves 1-2

To make this even tastier, add a stick of cheese, cut up, to the final dish. Make sure you mix all of the ingredients together very well or you may get big bites of paprika.

1 cup butter flavored mashed potatoes
6 packets True Lemon
4 tablespoons paprika (hot or sweet)
1 teaspoon parsley flakes

At home: combine all of the ingredients in a zip locking plastic bag.

In camp: add about 2 cups of hot water. Stir well and enjoy.

Bacon Broccoli Cheese Mashed Potatoes
Serves 1

1 cup butter flavored mashed potatoes
3 tablespoon broccoli cheddar soup mix
2 tablespoons shelf stable bacon bits
1 tablespoon dried broccoli
salt, pepper and olive oil to taste

At home: combine all of the ingredients in a zip locking plastic bag.

In camp: add about 2 cups of hot water. Stir well and enjoy.

Maple Bacon Fry Bread
Serves 2-4

1 package just-add-water biscuit mix
3 tablespoons maple syrup granules (available online)
2 tablespoons shelf stable bacon
vegetable oil

Combine all of the ingredients except for the vegetable oil. Add about 1/2 cup water and mix well. Let stand for 5 minutes (you will get a fluffier bread).

Heat skillet. Add just enough vegetable oil to coat the pan. Drop the batter in tablespoonfuls into the hot oil. Spread so the bread is no more than 1/4 inch thick. Fry until golden on both sides.

Cinnamon Raisin Bannock
Serves 2

1 ½ cups Bisquick
¼ cup raisins
¼ cup oatmeal
2 tablespoons almond meal
1 tablespoon white sugar
1 teaspoon ground cinnamon
Oil for frying

At home: combine all of the dry ingredients in a zip locking plastic bag. Carry the oil in a leak proof container.

In camp: add about 1 cup water to the bag and squish until well combined. Heat oil in your pan. Snip off one corner of the bag and squish out lumps of dough into the hot oil. Fry on both sides until golden brown and cooked through.

Mushroom Tomato Rice
Serves 1

¼ cup instant rice
2 tablespoons dried mushrooms
1 tablespoon dried tomatoes
½ teaspoon vegetable bouillon
¼ teaspoon dried thyme
salt, pepper and olive oil to taste

At home: combine all of the ingredients in a zip locking plastic bag.

In camp: add just enough hot water to cover. Stir well. Season to taste with salt, pepper and olive oil.

Tomato Herb Quinoa
Serves 1
2 ounces

1/3 cup cooked and dehydrated quinoa
2 tablespoons dried tomatoes
1 tablespoon dried mixed vegetables
½ teaspoon dried basil
½ teaspoon dried oregano
¼ teaspoon dried thyme
¼ teaspoon garlic powder
Parmesan cheese and olive oil to taste

At home: combine everything except the Parmesan and oil in a zip locking plastic bag.

In camp: add enough hot water to cover. Allow to stand until quinoa and vegetables are rehydrated. Top with Parmesan and stir in olive oil to taste.

Spicy Potatoes and Tomatoes
Serves 1
2 ounces

¼ cup dried potato dices or shreds
¼ cup dried tomato dices
1 tablespoon onion flakes
1 teaspoon parsley flakes
½ teaspoon ground cumin
½ teaspoon garlic powder
¼ teaspoon turmeric
1/8 teaspoon cayenne pepper
salt, pepper and olive oil to taste

At home: combine everything except oil in a zip locking plastic bag.

In camp: add enough hot water to cover and place in a cozy. Allow to sit until the vegetables are rehydrated. Stir in olive oil to taste.

Chapter 9 - Dinners

Dinners are the easiest meals for me to plan when I start thinking about my backcountry menu.

There is nothing better than sitting in camp as the sun is dipping below a nearby ridge, chatting with hiking friends and eating some sort of delicious concoction. In most cases, my dinner is eaten right out of a zip locking freezer bag.

Food at dinner helps keep you warm at night and replaces all those calories you burned during your day. Hiking is hard work and it is a great excuse to be able to eat a lot.

If I am eating dinner with a group of friends, it is time to catch up on their lives and gossip. If I am on a solo trip, dinner is a time to take in the scenery and reflect on my own life.

Choose a dinner that suits your style of cooking, be it freezer bag cooking, a one pan wonder or a multi-course meal. Look at the lunch recipes for no-cook dinner ideas.

Many of the dinner recipes call for pre-cooked and then dehydrated pasta, or quinoa. Feel free to substitute ramen or couscous to make these recipes dehydrator-free.

To make "instant" noodles, rice, or quinoa, cook as you normally would and then spread in a single layer on lined dehydrator trays. Dehydrate 4-8 hours at 135 degrees until there is no damp spots. I find that small pasta shapes (wheels, shells, spirals) work best for this type of backcountry cooking.

Please see the online sources list in the back of the book for ingredients such as dried lentils, beans, shelf stable and powdered cheeses and various dried meat products.

Greek Chicken and Rice
Serves 1

3 ounce can chicken (or 3 tablespoons dried)
1/3 cup instant rice
2 tablespoons dried vegetables
1 teaspoon dried oregano
1/2 teaspoon chicken bouillon
1/4 teaspoon garlic powder
2 packets True Lemon

At home: combine all the dry ingredients in a zip locking plastic bag. Carry the chicken separately.

In camp: place bag in a cozy. Add just enough water to cover. Let stand 5-10 minutes. Stir in the chicken (no need to drain) and serve.

Oysters and Rice
Serves 1-2

1/3 cup instant rice
1 can smoked oysters
1 teaspoon dried parsley
1/2 teaspoon vegetable bouillon
1/4 teaspoon Old Bay seasoning
1/4 teaspoon garlic powder

At home: combine all the dry ingredients in a zip locking plastic bag. Carry the oysters separately.

In camp: place bag in a cozy. Add just enough water to cover. Let stand 5-10 minutes. Stir in the oysters (no need to drain) and serve.

Lemon Dill Tuna and Rice
Serves 1

1/3 cup instant rice
1/2 teaspoon vegetable bouillon
1 tablespoon mixed dried vegetables
2 packets True Lemon
1 teaspoon dried dill
1 foil pouch tuna

At home: combine all the dry ingredients in a zip locking plastic bag. Carry the tuna separately.

In camp: place bag in a cozy. Place the foil pouch between the cozy and the bag to warm. Add just enough water to cover. Let stand 5-10 minutes. Stir in the tuna and serve.

Lemongrass and Ginger Rice with Salmon
Serves 1-2

1 foil pouch salmon
½ cup instant rice
3 tablespoons dried vegetables
2 tablespoons coconut crème powder
1 teaspoon dried lemongrass
½ teaspoon ground ginger
½ teaspoon vegetable bouillon
2 packets True Lime
Salt, pepper and olive oil to taste

At home: combine all of the dry ingredients in a zip locking plastic bag. Carry the olive oil in a screw top container.

In camp: add just enough hot or cold water to cover the rice. Allow to rehydrate, and then stir in the salmon, salt, pepper and olive oil.

Thai Mango Chicken and Rice
Serves 1

This recipe has seen a lot of trail time already. I have sent it with GoBlueHiker and Turtle on several trips and it is one of my favorites as well. Turtle insists that I make this for her on every trip we take.

3 ounce can chicken (or 3 tablespoons dried)
1/3 cup instant rice
3 tablespoons chopped dried mango
1 tablespoon dried roasted bell pepper
1 tablespoon coconut crème powder
1/2 teaspoon dried basil

At home: combine everything in a zip locking plastic bag. Carry the can of chicken separately. (If using dried chicken, add it with the dry ingredients)

In camp: place bag in a cozy. Add just enough water to cover. Let stand 5-10 minutes. Stir in the chicken and serve.

Orange Teriyaki Chicken and Rice
Serves 1

Freeze dried oranges and soy sauce powder are available online. You could substitute dried orange zest (about ½-1 teaspoon) for the freeze dried oranges.

3 tablespoons dried chicken
¼ cup instant rice
2 tablespoons freeze dried oranges
1 tablespoon dried peas
1 ½ teaspoons soy sauce powder (or 1 packet soy sauce)
1 teaspoon brown sugar
½ teaspoon ground ginger
¼ teaspoon dry mustard

At home: combine all of the ingredients in a zip locking plastic bag.

In camp: add just enough hot water to cover. Stir well and eat.

Chicken Almandine
Serves 1

This recipe was field tested for me in the Queets Rainforest by OlyHiker and GoBlueHiker.

3 tablespoons dried chicken (or 3 ounce can)
1/3 cup instant rice
2 tablespoons dried mushrooms
2 tablespoons powdered milk
1 tablespoon freeze dried green beans
1 teaspoon dried parsley
½ teaspoon dried celery
½ teaspoon dried chives
2-3 tablespoons chopped or slivered almonds

At home: combine everything but the almonds in a zip locking plastic bag. Place the almonds in a second bag.

In camp: add just enough hot water to cover. Stir well and place in a cozy. When the rice and vegetables are rehydrated, stir again and serve topped with the almonds.

Black Beans and Rice
Serves 1

You could add a few dashes of Tabasco to the rehydrated meal for more of a kick.

1/3 cup instant rice
1/3 cup dried black beans
3 tablespoons dried bell peppers
1 teaspoon dried cilantro
½ teaspoon chili powder
½ teaspoon onion flakes
¼ teaspoon garlic powder
pinch cayenne pepper

At home: combine everything in a zip locking plastic bag.

In camp: add enough hot water to cover. Allow to sit until rice and beans are rehydrated. Season with salt, pepper and olive oil to taste.

Green Tea Rice and Vegetables
Serves 1

1/3 cup instant rice
¼ cup dried mixed vegetables
2 tablespoons plain textured vegetable protein
¼ teaspoon ground ginger
1 ½ teaspoons unsweetened green tea powder
½ teaspoon vegetable bouillon

At home: combine everything in a zip locking plastic bag.

In camp: add enough hot water to cover. Allow to sit until the rice and vegetables are rehydrated. Season with salt, pepper and olive oil to taste.

Rice and Veggies with Peanut Sauce
Serves 1

This recipe was one of Rainrunner's favorite's when she thru-hiked the Pacific Crest Trail.

1/3 cup instant rice
3 tablespoons powdered peanut sauce mix
2 tablespoons coconut crème powder
3 tablespoons dried mixed vegetables
1-2 tablespoons plain textured vegetable protein (optional, but it adds extra protein and potassium)

At home: combine all of the ingredients in a zip locking plastic bag.

In camp: add enough hot water to cover, stir well and let sit until the rice is cooked and vegetables are rehydrated. Stir again before eating.

Ginger Coconut Rice and Sweet Potatoes
Serves 1

This is very tasty recipe. It would also make a nice, unusual, trail breakfast.

¼ cup dehydrated sweet potatoes
1/3 cup instant rice
1 teaspoon ground ginger
2 tablespoons coconut crème powder
2 tablespoons dried mixed vegetables
1 packet True Lime
2 teaspoons textured vegetable protein
¼ teaspoon onion flakes
Salt, pepper and olive oil to taste

At home: combine everything in a zip locking plastic bag.

In camp: add enough hot water to cover. Allow to sit until rice is soft and vegetables are rehydrated. Season with salt, pepper and olive oil to taste.

Pasta Morena
Serves 1

1/3 cup cooked and dehydrated pasta
2 tablespoon country gravy mix
1 tablespoon dried peas
1 tablespoon powdered milk
1 tablespoon dried mushrooms
1 teaspoon shelf stable bacon bits

At home: combine everything in a zip locking plastic bag.

In camp: add enough hot water to cover (about a cup). Stir well, making sure you get all the powdered ingredients out of the corners. Place in a cozy for 5 minutes. Stir again before eating.

Eagle Creek Stroganoff
Serves 1

My carnivore husband tested this for me. Gravy, meat and noodles... What's not to love?

Dried mushrooms and/or tomatoes would be an excellent addition to this. Use potato slices instead of noodles for a variation.

1/2 cup cooked and dehydrated noodles
1/4 cup freeze dried beef
2 tablespoons dry brown gravy mix
2 tablespoons dried mixed vegetables
1 tablespoon powdered milk
1/4 teaspoon paprika
1/4 teaspoon Italian herb seasoning blend
1/8 teaspoon garlic powder

At home: combine everything in a zip locking plastic bag.

In camp: add enough hot water to cover (about a cup). Stir well, making sure you get all the powdered ingredients out of the corners. Place in a cozy for 5 minutes. Stir again before eating.

Pasta with Creamy Mushroom Sauce
Serves 1

I developed this recipe by special request for Spindle. She gave me the framework and I created the recipe for her. You must like mushrooms for this one! I use a blend of creminis, button and oyster mushrooms.

1/2 cup cooked and dehydrated pasta
2 tablespoons mushroom sauce
3 tablespoons dried mushrooms
1 tablespoon dried mixed vegetables
1 tablespoon powdered milk
1/4 teaspoon garlic powder

At home: combine all of the ingredients in a zip locking plastic bag.

In camp: add enough hot water to cover (about 1 cup). Place bag in a freezer bag cozy and allow to rehydrate. Stir well before eating.

Creamy Salmon Carbonara
Serves 1

A version of this recipe was featured in Backpacker Magazine January 2011 as a Reader's Choice Award winner. It is also Squatch's (walkpct.com) favorite.

½ cup cooked and dehydrated pasta
1 foil pouch salmon
2 tablespoons shelf stable bacon
2 tablespoons powdered eggs
1 tablespoon powdered milk
1 tablespoon powdered cheese
1 tablespoon white sauce or gravy mix
1 teaspoon sun dried tomatoes, finely chopped (about 1 whole tomato)

At home: combine all of the ingredients except the salmon in a zip locking plastic bag.

In camp: add just enough hot water to cover. Stir well and place in a cozy. When the pasta is rehydrated, stir in the salmon and eat.

Mushrooms Paprikash
Serves 1

1/3 cup cooked and dehydrated pasta
¼ cup dried mushrooms
1 tablespoon dried tomatoes
1 teaspoon smoked paprika
1 teaspoon dried bell pepper
½ teaspoon onion flakes
¼ teaspoon garlic powder
1 packet shelf stable cream cheese

At home: combine everything except the cheese in a zip locking plastic bag. Carry the cheese separately (the paprika sticks to the packaging too much if you don't).

In camp: add just enough hot water to cover. Place bag in a cozy and allow the pasta and mushrooms to rehydrate. Stir in the cream cheese just before eating.

Creamy Pesto Noodles with Veggies
Serves 1-2

1 ½ cups cooked and dehydrated pasta
1 package creamy pesto sauce mix
1/3 cup powdered milk
1 tablespoon butter powder
¼ cup dried vegetables

At home: combine everything in a zip locking plastic bag.

In camp: add enough hot water to cover. Allow to sit until pasta is soft and vegetables are rehydrated. Season with salt, pepper and olive oil to taste.

Pasta ala Squatch
Serves 1

This tastes like home made tuna casserole!

¼ cup broccoli cheese soup mix
½ cup cooked and dehydrated pasta
2 tablespoons dried broccoli
1 tablespoon powdered milk
1 foil pouch tuna

At home: combine everything except the tuna in a zip locking plastic bag.

In camp: add enough hot water to cover. Stir well. Place in a cozy with the tuna. Let stand for 5-10 minutes. Stir in the tuna and eat hot.

Variation: add 2-3 tablespoons shelf stable bacon.

Couscous with Lemon, Chicken and Peas
Serves 1

1/3 cup couscous
2 tablespoons dried chicken
2 tablespoons dried peas
2 packets True Lemon
1 teaspoon chicken bouillon

At home: combine everything in a zip locking plastic bag.

In camp: add enough hot water to cover. Stir well, making sure you get all the powdered ingredients out of the corners. Place in a cozy for 5 minutes. Stir again before eating.

Chickpea Couscous Marinara
Serves 2

Spindle field tested this for me while climbing 14'ers in Colorado. She served it with a bit of garlic naan and some mint tea.

1/4 cup couscous
1/4 cup (cooked or canned) dehydrated chickpeas
1 tablespoon onion flakes
1 teaspoon parsley flakes
1/2 teaspoon dried oregano
1/2 teaspoon dried basil
1/2 teaspoon dried thyme
1/4 teaspoon garlic powder (or more, to taste)
2 tablespoons dried tomatoes
2 tablespoons tomato powder
1 teaspoon sugar
salt and pepper to taste
2-4 Parmesan cheese packets

At home: combine everything except the cheese in a zip locking plastic bag.

In camp: Add just enough water to cover. Stir and allow to rehydrate. Serve topped with Parmesan.

Lentils and Couscous
Serves 1

This dish is very simple, but very satisfying.

¼ cup cooked and dehydrated lentils
¼ cup couscous
1 tablespoon dried tomatoes
1 tablespoon dried bell peppers
1 teaspoon dried parsley
1 teaspoon vegetable bouillon
½ teaspoon onion flakes
¼ teaspoon dried oregano
1 packet True Lemon

At home: combine everything in a zip locking plastic bag.

In camp: add enough hot water to cover. Allow to sit until lentils are rehydrated. Season with salt, pepper and olive oil to taste.

Chicken Mushroom Cheese Couscous
Serves 1

1/3 cup couscous
2 tablespoon dried mushrooms
2 tablespoons cheddar cheese powder
1 tablespoon dried chicken (or a small can/pouch)
1 tablespoon dried peas (or vegetable of your choice)
1/2 teaspoon chicken or vegetable bullion

At home: combine all of the ingredients in a zip locking plastic bag.

In camp: add hot water to cover. Stir well, place in a cozy and allow to stand for 5 minutes. Stir again before eating.

Bean and Cheese Couscous
Serves 1

I served this dinner to a bunch of hungry Pacific Crest Trail thru hikers. They were raving about how good it was. On the other hand, maybe they were just hungry.

1/3 cup cooked and dehydrated black beans
1/3 cup couscous
2 tablespoons cheese powder
½ teaspoon vegetable bouillon
½ teaspoon dry mustard powder
¼ teaspoon onion flakes
¼ teaspoon dried oregano

At home: combine all of the ingredients in a zip locking plastic bag.

In camp: add just enough hot water to cover. Stir well. Place in a cozy and let stand for 5 minutes or until the beans and couscous are rehydrated.

Queets Valley Shepherd's Pie
Serves 2-4

This recipe can easily be divided in half. Just use half of everything and adjust water amounts accordingly.

I developed this recipe to feed a group of hungry hikers who were seeing GoBlueHiker off on one of his grand adventures. It was later featured in Backpacker Magazine as a Reader's Choice Award Winner.

7 ounce package baked tofu
4 ounce package buttery home-style mashed potatoes
1 packet mushroom sauce
1/2 cup dried mushrooms
1/4 cup dried mixed vegetables
1/2 teaspoon vegetable bouillon
1/4 teaspoon dried sage
1/2 teaspoon dried thyme
salt and pepper to taste

At home: combine the vegetables, sage, thyme, and bouillon in a zip locking plastic bag. Label "add 1 cup water". In a second zip locking plastic bag, place the potatoes. Label "add 2 cups water". Carry the mushroom sauce and tofu separately.

In camp: bring 3 cups water to a boil. Meanwhile, Dice the tofu. 2 cups of water go to the potatoes. 1 cup water to the vegetables. Place both bags in a freezer bag cozy (or two!)

Meanwhile, while the vegetables are rehydrating, sauté the tofu in a little olive oil (just getting it heated through). Turn off the heat. Add the vegetables. Do not drain. You want it a little wet. Add the packet of mushroom sauce and stir well. It will thicken a little. Top with the mashed potatoes before serving.

Citrus Lentils with Salmon
Serves 1-2

High protein! High flavor!

1 foil pouch salmon
1/3 cup (cooked and dehydrated) lentils
1/4 cup dried vegetables
1/2 teaspoon vegetable bouillon
2 packets True Orange
2 packets True Lemon
Salt, pepper and olive oil to taste

At home: combine all of the dry ingredients in a zip locking plastic bag. Carry the olive oil in a screw top container.

In camp: add just enough hot or cold water to cover the lentils. Allow to rehydrate, and then stir in the salmon, salt, pepper and olive oil.

Goblin's Gate Lentils
Serves 1

1/4 cup cooked and dehydrated lentils
1 tablespoon onion flakes
2 tablespoons dried carrots
1/4 teaspoon thyme
1/4 teaspoon oregano
1/2 teaspoon vegetable bullion
1 teaspoon dried parsley
2 tablespoons dried tomatoes
1-2 packets of Parmesan cheese, to taste

At home: combine all of the ingredients, except the cheese, in a zip locking plastic bag. Carry the cheese separately.

In camp: add 1/2 to 3/4 cup boiling water to the lentils. Stir and allow to rehydrate. Top with Parmesan cheese and serve.

Lentil Joes
Serves 1-2

A big thank you goes out to Hoosierdaddy, who tested this dish for me, not once, but three times. I still didn't add the meat like he wanted, but he was instrumental in developing the final recipe. Stir very well before eating as the spices tend to sink to the bottom.

1/3 cup cooked and dried lentils
2 tablespoons dried tomatoes
3 tablespoons textured vegetable protein
1 tablespoon tomato powder
1 tablespoon onion flakes
1 tablespoon dried bell pepper
1 tablespoon dried mushrooms
1 tablespoon chili powder
2 teaspoons brown sugar
½ teaspoon dry mustard
½ teaspoon garlic powder
pinch cayenne (or more to taste)
salt to taste

At home: combine everything in a zip locking plastic bag.

In camp: add enough hot water to cover. Stir well and place in a cozy. Let stand for 5 minutes or until the lentils are tender. Stir again before eating.

Chapter 10 - Desserts

Desserts can be as simple or as complicated as you want to make them. Shelf stable pudding cups are a great choice for one or two night trips and are a huge hit with the kids. There are lots of trail friendly cookies available right off the grocery store shelves.

Dessert does not always have to follow dinner. Sometimes you need a little pick me up in the middle of the day to get up that giant hill. My food bag always contains dried mangos and dark chocolate. I dip into my treats as needed.

On trips of four or more people, I insist on bringing and making dessert; usually some sort of pie or cheesecake. It is fun to share! My hiking partners get dishwashing duty though.

While desserts are not necessary in your meal planning, they are a nice addition and a great way to get in lots of extra needed calories. If your dinner is lacking, or was less filling than you expected, desserts can add the needed calories to keep you satisfied. Hiking is hard work. Eat dessert without guilt. You've earned it!

Banana Walnut Pudding
Serves 4

Team Osbourne field tested this for me on a backpacking trip through the Enchantments.

1 box instant banana pudding
1 cup powdered milk
1/4 cup freeze dried bananas
1/4 cup chopped walnuts

At home: combine the milk and pudding mix in a zip locking plastic bag. Combine the bananas and walnuts in a second bag.

In camp: add 3 cups of cold water to the pudding mix. Squish the bag until there are no dry spots and the pudding is well mixed. Serve topped with the freeze-dried bananas and walnuts.

Banana Rice Pudding
Serves 1

You don't want to smash the bananas into crumbs, just small pieces. The cornstarch helps to thicken this to a pudding like consistency.

½ cup instant rice
½ cup freeze dried bananas, lightly crushed
¼ cup powdered milk
2 tablespoons brown sugar
1 tablespoon corn starch
½ teaspoon cinnamon
1/8 teaspoon ground nutmeg

At home: combine all of the ingredients in a zip locking plastic bag. Make sure you mix well or the ingredients tend to clump with the brown sugar.

In camp: add hot water to cover. Place in a cozy and let sit for 5-10 minutes. Stir well and serve warm.

Variation: instead of the brown sugar, cinnamon and nutmeg, stir in 2 tablespoons of maple syrup.

Vanilla Green Tea Mousse
Serves 2

A fun green dessert. This one is not overly sweet.

1 box vanilla mousse mix
1/3 cup powdered milk
1 1/2 tablespoons instant green tea powder

At home: combine all of the dry ingredients in a zip locking plastic bag. Label the bag "add 1 cup cold water."

In camp: add 1 cup of cold water to the bag. Squish to combine, making sure there are no dry spots. Allow to set. Eat!

Double Raspberry Chocolate Mousse
Serves 2-4

Dried raspberries are available in some grocery stores now! They are a bit spendy, but delicious!! This would also be tasty with frangelico or amaretto added.

1 raspberry chocolate mousse mix
1/3 cup powdered milk
1/4 cup dried raspberries (not freeze-dried, but those would work)
1/4 cup mini chocolate chips

At home: combine the mousse mix and milk in a zip locking plastic bag. Combine the raspberries and chocolate chips in a second bag.

In camp: add 1 cup of cold water to the mousse mix. Squish to combine, making sure there are no dry spots. Allow to set. Top with the chocolate and raspberries. Eat!

Almond Joy Mousse
Serves 2

GoBlueHiker field tested this for me on one of his Queets Valley trips.

1 package Dark Chocolate Truffle Mousse (or other chocolate flavor) mix
¼ cup powdered milk
3 tablespoons coconut crème powder
2 tablespoons slivered almonds
2 tablespoons shredded coconut

At home: combine the mousse mix, powdered milk and coconut crème powder in a zip locking plastic bag. Carry the almonds and coconut in a second, smaller bag.

In camp: add 1 cup cold water. Squish the bag to get rid of any dry spots. Serve topped with the almonds and shredded coconut.

Mocha Mousse Pie
Serves 2-4

1 graham cracker crust from an instant cheesecake mix*
1 package chocolate mousse mix
1/3 cup powdered milk
2 tablespoons instant coffee
Olive oil
10 chocolate covered espresso beans (or more to taste)

At home: combine the mousse mix, powdered milk and instant coffee in a zip locking plastic bag. Leave the crust mix in the bag it came in. Place the espresso beans in a second bag. Carry the olive oil in a leak proof container.

In camp: pour the crust mix into the bottom of your pan and add enough oil to make the crumbs stick together. Press the crumbs along the bottoms and the sides of the pan, as evenly as possible.

Add about 1 cup of cold water to the mousse mix and squish the bag until there are no visible lumps and the mixture is well combined. Pour the mousse onto the crust, spreading it out evenly. Let stand for a couple of minutes to set up.

Garnish with chocolate covered espresso beans.

* Use the cheesecake mix to make the following recipe.

Chocolate Cherry Cheesecake
Serves 4-6

1 cup chocolate cookie crumbs
1 box instant cheesecake mix with cherry topping
1/4 cup cocoa powder
1/2 cup powdered milk
3-4 Tablespoons olive oil or butter

At home: Set the crust from the mix aside for another recipe. put filling mix, powdered milk and cocoa powder in a zip locking plastic bag. Place the cookie crumbs in second bag. Leave the cherry topping in its own bag. Carry the olive oil in a leak proof container.

In camp: add 1 1/2 cups water to the cheesecake mix. Close the bag and squish until there are no dry lumps of mix. Meanwhile, combine olive oil and cookie crumbs. Mix well. Spread as evenly as possible over the bottom and sides of the pan. Top with cheesecake mix. Allow to set. Top with cherry topping.

Margarita Cheesecake
Serves 4

A margarita flavored Jell-O does exist, but it is a seasonal flavor and can be difficult to find. Yes, your cheesecake will be green. It's festive!

1 package instant cheesecake mix
1 package lime Jell-O
1/2 cup powdered milk
1 mini bottle tequila
1/4 cup crushed salted pretzels

At home: combine the cheesecake mix, Jell-O and powdered milk in a zip locking plastic bag. In a second bag, combine the pretzels and 1/4 cup of the crust mix.

Use the remaining (about 3/4 cup) crust mix for another recipe.

In camp: add enough water to the tequila to equal 1 1/2 cups. Mix this with your cheesecake/Jell-O mixture in your pan. Let sit for a minute or two, and then top with the pretzels/crust mix.

Bailey's Vanilla Mousse Tarts
Serves 4

This dessert is extremely rich.

1 box instant vanilla mousse mix
1/3 cup powdered milk
1 mini bottle Bailey's Irish Cream
1 1-½ ounce package chocolate fudge topping
4 mini graham cracker tart shells

At home: combine chocolate mousse mix and powdered milk in a zip locking plastic bag. Carry the fudge topping, tart shells and Irish Cream separately.

In camp: add the Irish Cream and enough water to total 1 cup liquid (about ¾ cup water – use less liquor for a milder flavor). Stir well and set aside until firmed up. Meanwhile open the chocolate fudge topping and divide it as evenly as possible between the four tart shells. Top with the mousse and enjoy.

Elvis Pie
Serves 2

2 mini graham cracker crust pie shells
2 snack packs banana pudding
1 single serving size peanut butter, or about 2 tablespoons
2 teaspoons chocolate chips

Spread half of the peanut butter on each of the pie shells. Top with a cup of the pudding and 1 tablespoon each of the chocolate chips. Enjoy!

Variations - use one idea or a combination of all of them!

Nutella instead of peanut butter
Vanilla pudding instead of banana
Chopped nuts instead of chocolate chips

Note: If you don't want to use the mini graham cracker crusts, crushed vanilla wafers or graham crackers in the bottom of your bowl would work just as well. Or Oreos. Or whatever your favorite cookie is. Get creative! Have fun and eat well!

Spiced Pear Tart
Serves 1

1 mini graham cracker crust pie shell
1 package shelf stable cream cheese
3 tablespoons dried pears, chopped
1 teaspoon ground cinnamon
1 teaspoon brown sugar
½ teaspoon ground ginger
¼ teaspoon ground nutmeg

At home: combine the pears and spices in a zip locking plastic bag. Carry the graham cracker crust and cream cheese separately.

In camp: add just enough hot or cold water to cover the pears. Set aside and allow to rehydrate. Meanwhile spread the cream cheese in the bottom and up the sides of the graham cracker crust. When the pears are rehydrated, stir well and spoon over the cream cheese.

Hubby Parfait
Serves 1

1/4 cup Nutter Butters or other peanut butter filled cookie
1 snack pack vanilla pudding

At home: place everything in a bag.

In camp: crush cookies if they are not already crushed. Layer the crushed cookies alternately with the vanilla pudding in your cup or bowl.

Variation: try this with banana or chocolate pudding.

Coconut Cheesecake Dip
Serves 1

1 package shelf stable cream cheese
2 tablespoons coconut crème powder
1 teaspoon white sugar
cookies and/or fruit for dipping

At home: combine the coconut crème powder and sugar in a bag. Carry the cookies and cream cheese in a second bag.

In camp: add the cream cheese to the coconut crème powder. Squish the bag until well combined. Spread on cookies or dip fruit to serve

Cran-Apple "Cheesecake"
Serves 1-2

1 mini graham cracker crust (or 2-3 graham crackers)
1 package shelf stable cream cheese
1/8 cup dried apples, diced
1/8 cup dried cranberries
1 teaspoon brown sugar
½ teaspoon crystallized ginger, chopped
½ teaspoon ground cinnamon

At home: crumble the graham cracker crust. Combine everything in a zip locking plastic bag. Do not open the cream cheese.

In camp: add the cream cheese to the dry ingredients. Seal the bag and squish until well combined. Serve.

Chapter 11 - S'mores

At the ALDHA-West Gathering a few years ago, I bought a bag of ingredients to experiment with at the bonfire. Here are some of the delicious results.

Chocolate Strawberry S'mores
Serves 3

6 chocolate shortbread cookies
1 package shelf stable strawberry cream cheese
3 marshmallows

At home: put the graham cookies and marshmallows in a zip locking plastic bag. Carry the cream cheese separately.

In camp: toast the marshmallows over your stove or campfire. Spread half of the cream cheese on each of two cookies. Top with toasted marshmallows then the other two cookies. Smoosh and eat.

Chocolate Peanut Butter S'mores
Serves 1

4 chocolate shortbread cookies
2-4 large marshmallows (depends on your taste and size of cookies)
2 ounce peanut butter

At home: put the shortbread cookies and marshmallows in a zip locking plastic bag. Carry the peanut butter separately.

In camp: find a stick (from a non-poisonous plant!) and toast the marshmallows over your stove or campfire. Spread half of the peanut butter on each of two cookies. Top with toasted marshmallows, then the other two cookies. Smoosh and eat.

Full Monty S'mores
Serves 1

4 graham crackers
2-4 large marshmallows (depends on your taste and size of cookies)
2 pieces dark chocolate
1 package shelf stable cream cheese

At home: put the graham crackers, chocolate and marshmallows in a zip locking plastic bag. Carry the cream cheese separately.

In camp: toast the marshmallows over your stove or campfire. Spread half of the cream cheese on each of two graham crackers. Top with toasted marshmallows, the chocolate and then the other two graham crackers. Smoosh and eat.

Half Mile S'mores
Serves 1

4 gingersnap cookies
2 tablespoons lemon curd
2 large marshmallows

At home: put the cookies and marshmallows in a zip locking plastic bag. Carry the lemon curd in a leak proof container.

In camp: toast the marshmallows over your stove or campfire. Spread two of the cookies with 1 tablespoon lemon curd. Top with toasted marshmallows and the other two cookies.

Dicentra S'mores
Serves 1

As seen in Backpacker Magazine, online.

4 slices fresh pear
2 large marshmallows
4 graham crackers
1 tablespoon Nutella

At home: put the graham crackers and marshmallows in a zip locking plastic bag. Carry the Nutella and pear separately.

In camp: toast the marshmallows over your stove or campfire. Spread half of the Nutella on each of two graham crackers. Top with toasted marshmallows, the pear slices and then the other two graham crackers.

Chapter 12 - Cooking with Kids

Kids are notoriously picky eaters. When I'm asked what to serve kids on the trail, I always recommend serving them what they like to eat at home. Macaroni and cheese is usually a big hit.

I also like making the food fun for them. Have little treats or special snacks available. Fun or gross names for your meals can encourage kids to eat too. That isn't spaghetti in your bowl; it's worms! Those aren't dried cranberries, they are fire ants. Get them involved in the food planning and shopping and they are more likely to eat what they are served.

Now that I'm packing a school lunch each day for my Little Monkey, I'm finding a lot of things that would also work for hiking and backpacking. There are a ton of things that are already designed to stand up to being banged around in a lunch box without refrigeration.

Foods that my daughter like include mini bagels, mini sandwich thins, quesadillas, salami, cheese & crackers, cheese sticks, pretzels, mashed potatoes, dry sweetened cereals (think of it as trail mix), nuts and dried fruits. Her favorites are dried cranberries and mangos. She flips out over plain Top Ramen. We call them "yarn noodles." Boiled quails eggs are also a huge hit. They taste like regular boiled eggs, but with an added cuteness factor.

Banana Nutella Mini Bagels
Serves 1

1 whole wheat mini bagel
¼ small fresh banana
1 tablespoon Nutella (or a single serving packet)

At home: wrap the bagel and banana in foil. Place the Nutella in a screw top or other airtight container.

In camp: split the bagel in half. Spread both sides of the bagel with Nutella. Peel and slice the banana and sandwich between the bagel halves.

Berry Bagels
Serves 1

Let the kids dot on the berries before eating.

1 blueberry mini bagel
1 package shelf stable strawberry cream cheese
1 tablespoon dried cranberries, cherries or blueberries

At home: wrap the bagel in foil. Carry the dried fruit in a small zip locking plastic bag.

In camp: split the bagel in half. Spread both sides of the bagel with cream cheese. Top with the dried berries and press both halves of the bagel together before eating.

Veggie Dippers

This is more of a concept than a recipe. Kids love dipping stuff!
Choose their favorite vegetable and dip. Single serving sized
packets of salad dressing and salsa are available online and at
some fast food places.

The vegetables:
mini carrots or carrot sticks
snap peas
jicama sticks
green beans, trimmed
bell peppers, cut in sticks
celery sticks
radishes
daikon, cut in slices or sticks
snow peas
cauliflower or broccoli florets
zucchini or yellow squash slices or sticks

Dip in:
hummus
peanut butter or other nut butters
ketchup
ranch dressing or other salad dressings
salsa
applesauce
mustard or honey mustard
barbecue sauce
bean dip or refried beans
cream cheese or other soft cheese spreads

Ants on a Log

Another concept as opposed to a recipe. I'm sure you've seen this before.

Stuff celery sticks (or spread crackers) with:

peanut butter or other nut butters
cream cheese (flavored or plain)
goat cheese
refried beans
hummus
Cheese Wiz

Then topped with:

raisins
marshmallows
olives
bacon bits
fried onions, broken up
various nuts or seeds
sun dried tomatoes
dried cranberries or other dried fruit (chopped up)

Variations:

fire ants on a log – use sun dried tomatoes or dried cranberries
pine beetles on a log – use pine nuts
green beetles on a log – use pistachios
grubs on a log – use marshmallows

Caramel Apple Dippers
Serves 1-2

I especially like the chocolate caramel dip for this recipe. Look for it in the produce section of your local grocery store. This is also very good with pears, but they do not travel as well as apples. Cut them in camp.

1 small tart apple, cut in wedges
1 ounce container caramel dip

At home: place the apples in a zip locking plastic bag. For convenience, you can put the caramel container right in the bag.

In camp: open the caramel dip and dunk the apples.

Glossary

Bacon, Shelf Stable – Dried bacon bits may be substituted, but the flavor will not be the same. Look for shelf stable bacon in the salad dressing aisle, usually with the croutons and other salad toppers. Most brands recommend refrigeration after opening.

Beans, Dried – Look for "soup mixes" in the bulk bins. Also available online.

Bulgur – Look for it in bulk bins and "natural" food aisles. Substitute rice or cous cous in most instances.

Coconut Crème Powder – Available at Asian markets.

Coffee, Instant – There are so many choices for coffee now. Some are a lot better than others. Pick a good brand of instant coffee and you won't be sorry.

Cous Cous – Look for it in bulk bins or "natural" foods aisles. Often found with rice mixes. I only use plain (not flavored or seasoned). Bulgur or instant rice make good substitutes, but cooking time may need to be adjusted.

Five Spice Powder – A combination of spices, usually star anise, ginger, cloves, cinnamon, and either peppercorns or fennel seeds. Recipes vary. It is available in bulk spice bins, in the spice or Asian food aisles of larger supermarkets, Asian grocery stores or online. You can also make your own blend from the individual spices.

Fruit, Dried – There are a lot of choices available; dried, freeze-dried, chocolate coated, yogurt covered. Trader Joe's is my favorite place to buy dried fruit. If that isn't an option for you, try the bulk bins or baking aisle. You can also find freeze-dried fruit online at Harmony House Foods or Just Tomatoes.

Meats and Seafood – In foil pouches or cans. Try the tuna and/or canned meats aisles of your grocery store. Chicken may not be in the same aisle as tuna.

Milk, Powdered – I almost exclusively use Nido. It is a full fat powdered milk, and in my opinion, tastes a lot better than low fat powdered milk. It is available online at a variety of places or in the Hispanic food aisles of larger grocery stores.

Mushrooms, Dried – There are several varieties available, ranging in price from ridiculously priced to very affordable. Shiitakes are available at Asian markets, larger grocery stores (Asian foods aisle) and online. Gourmet mushrooms are available in larger grocery stores or online.

Nutella – Chocolate hazelnut spread, the consistency of peanut butter, which it makes a good substitute for. Peanut butter is an adequate substitute in some cases. It is found in larger grocery stores, usually with the peanut butter. Trader Joe's and some import stores also carry it.

Nuts and Seeds – There are a lot of choices available. I like to get mine either in bulk bins or at Trader Joes. They are also found in the baking aisle of most supermarkets. Seasoned varieties are appearing on the market now too. They add fat and protein to your meals without adding a whole lot of extra weight. Try different nuts than my recipes call for to add variety to your menus. Pecans instead of walnuts, pine nuts in place of almonds. Your choices are virtually endless.

Tortillas – Readily found in most supermarkets. Try some of the "gourmet" flavors that are available now.

Tofu – There are many types available. I like the shelf-stable kind (Mori-Nu brand) or the extra firm, refrigerated types – usually found in the produce section. I don't buy the type swimming in a lot of water. For dinner dishes, I use the firmer tofu. For desserts, such as puddings, I will use the softer, shelf stable variety. Baked tofu is excellent too. Try adding it to wraps or instant rice.

Tomatoes, Dried – See also, vegetables. There are two kinds of dried tomatoes; sun dried and freeze dried. Sun dried tomatoes are easier to find in grocery stores. Usually they are in the pasta aisle with the sauces.

Tomato, Powder – Available online and in bulk bins. It has a lot of flavor so a little bit goes a long way.

True Lemon/Lime/Orange – Substitute 1 teaspoon citrus juice or zest per packet. Available online at True Lemon and minimus.biz

TVP - Textured Vegetable Protein. I use plain, unflavored. Available in bulk bins, Natural food stores, "natural" food aisles or online. If you aren't used to eating TVP, start with small amounts as it can cause digestive issues.

Vegetables, Dried – Look for "soup mix" or Knorr soups. Also available online from Harmony House foods or Just Tomatoes.

Online Resources

Just Veggies: http://www.justtomatoes.com/
Freeze-dried vegetables and fruits with NOTHING added.

Harmony House Foods:
http://www.harmonyhousefoods.com/mainhome.html
All kinds of dried ingredients. Vegetables, beans, tomato powder,
soup blends, tvp, variety packs especially for backpackers.

King Arthur Flour: http://kingarthurflour.com/
This is really a site for bakers, but there is so much here that
works for backpackers! Specialty flours and sweeteners,
cornmeal, powdered eggs, buttermilk, cheese powder, spices,
flavorings, candied and dried fruit, nuts and more.

Minimus: http://www.minimus.biz/
This is a great website to buy vinegars, oils, sauces, True Lemon
and a hundred other things in single serving packages.

Pack It Gourmet: http://www.packitgourmet.com/
Meals and ingredients for backcountry cooking. Unusual
powdered products, drink mixes.

True Lemon: http://www.truelemon.com/
Makers of True Lemon, Lime and Orange. You can order the
packets from their site.

About the Author

Teresa "Dicentra" Black is a Northwest native who grew up camping and hiking all over Washington and Oregon. She is the co-founder of the local hiking group, Pacific Northwest Hikers.

Dicentra has served as the President and board member of the American Long Distance Hiking Association West. She is not a thru hiker, but she stays heavily involved with the thru hiker community.

She has backpacked and hiked in eight states. She lives in the Seattle area with her husband and daughter. Apart from cooking and the outdoors, her other hobbies include photography, reading, gardening, travel and knitting.

Her work has been seen in various publications, including the ALDHA-West Gazette and Backpacker Magazine.

This is her second book.

Index

Almond Joy Mousse 115
American River Sunshine Salad 61
Ants on a Log 129
Apple Cinnamon Oatmeal 28
Asian Mushroom Soup 76
Athenos Wrap 41
Backpacker's Quinoa Soup with Avocado and Corn 70
Bacon
    Bacon Broccoli Cheese Mashed Potatoes 83
    Bacon Mushroom Ramen 80
    Maple Bacon Fry Bread 84
    Pasta Morena 97
Bacon Broccoli Cheese Mashed Potatoes 83
Bacon Mushroom Ramen 80
Bagels
    Banana Nutella Mini Bagels 127
    Berry Bagels 127
    Heybrook Bagel 43
Bailey's Vanilla Mousse Tarts 119
Banana Nutella Mini Bagels 127
Banana Rice Pudding 113
Banana Walnut Pudding 112
Bean and Cheese Couscous 106
Beans
    Bean and Cheese Couscous 106
    Black Bean and Corn Salad 64
    Black Bean and Sweet Potato Chili 74
    Black Beans and Rice 94
    Black White and Red Chili 73
    Cheesy Black Bean Mashed Potatoes 82
    Vegetarian White Bean Chili 75
    White Bean and Fennel Salad 60
Beef
    Eagle Creek Stroganoff 98

Beef Stroganoff Ramen 79
BeeMan Hot Toddy 23
Berry Bagels 127
Berry Blend Gorp 49
Beverages 15
Black Bean and Corn Salad..64
Black Bean and Sweet Potato Chili 74
Black Beans and Rice...94
Black White and Red Chili 73
Breads and Sides 81
Breakfast 25
Bulgur
    Cran-Orange Breakfast Bulgur 30
    Lentil Bulgur Salad...62
Cali Wrap...41
Caramel Apple Dippers 130
Carrot Cake Oatmeal...27
Cheesy Black Bean Mashed Potatoes 82
Cherry Peach Couscous...29
Cherry Vanilla Chai 18
Chicken
    Chicken Almandine...93
    Chicken Curry Quinoa Salad...63
    Chicken Mushroom Cheese Couscous 105
    Coconut Curry Chicken Ramen...78
    Couscous with Lemon Chicken and Peas...............................103
    Greek Chicken and Rice..88
    Instant Chicken Curry Soup 71
    Orange Teriyaki Chicken and Rice 92
    Thai Mango Chicken and Rice...91
Chicken Almandine..93
Chicken Curry Quinoa Salad..63
Chicken Mushroom Cheese Couscous 105
Chicken Ramen Soup 77
Chickpea Couscous Marinara 104
Chili

Black Bean and Sweet Potato Chili 74
Black White and Red Chili 73
Vegetarian White Bean Chili 75
Chili Cheese Mashed Potatoes...82
Chocolate Cherry Cheesecake 117
Chocolate Peanut Butter S'mores 124
Chocolate Strawberry S'mores 123
Cinnamon Raisin Bannock 84
Citrus Lentils with Salmon 108
Cocktails
    BeeMan Hot Toddy 23
    Green Mountain Martini..24
    Springer Mountain Cooler 23
    X-Rated Lemonade 22
Coconut Chai 18
Coconut Cheesecake Dip 122
Coconut Curry Chicken Ramen 78
Coconut Ginger Couscous...29
Coconut Ginger Smoothie 16
Couscous
    American River Sunshine Salad 61
    Backpacker's Quinoa Soup...70
    Bean and Cheese Couscous 106
    Cherry Peach Couscous 29
    Chicken Mushroom Cheese Couscous 105
    Chickpea Couscous Marinara...104
    Coconut Ginger Couscous 29
    Couscous with Lemon Chicken and Peas.............................103
    Lentils and Couscous...105
Couscous with Lemon, Chicken and Peas 103
Cran-Apple "Cheesecake 122
Cran-Orange Breakfast Bulgur...30
Creamsicle Smoothie 17
Creamy Pesto Noodles with Veggies 101
Desserts 111
Dicentra S'mores 125

Dilly Tuna Salad 59
Dinners 87
Dips
    Ginger Curry Hummus 46
    Lentil Tapenade 45
    Mexicalli Hummus 47
    White Blaze Salmon Dip 44
Double Almond Pancakes 32
Double Raspberry Chocolate Mousse 114
Eagle Creek Stroganoff 98
Eggs
    McMountain Breakfast Sandwich 36
    Potato Egg Scramble 35
Elvis Pie 120
Esmeralda Wrap 39
ET's Mix 48
Fancy Gorp 49
Five Spice Peanuts 52
Full Monty S'mores 124
Ginger Coconut Rice and Sweet Potatoes 96
Ginger Curry Hummus 46
Ginger Peanuts 53
Glossary 131
Goblin's Gate Lentils 109
Greek Chicken and Rice 88
Green Mountain Martini 24
Green Tea Rice and Vegetables 95
Half Mile S'mores 125
Hazelnut Almond Mocha 21
Herbed Vegetable Broth 72
Heybrook Bagel 43
Hoosierdaddy's Grits 33
Hubby Parfait 121
Instant Chicken Curry Soup 71
It's in the Bag Trail Salad 58
Kids 126

Latte Bars 56
Lemon Dill Tuna and Rice...89
Lemon Dill Tuna Ramen..78
Lemon Paprika Mashed Potatoes.............................83
Lemongrass and Ginger Rice with Salmon 90
Lentil Bulgur Salad 62
Lentil Joes..110
Lentil Tapenade 45
Lentils
    Citrus Lentils with Salmon.................................108
    Goblin's Gate Lentils 109
    Lentils and Couscous...105
    Lentils Joes 110
    Tomato Basil Lentil Soup......................................67
Lentils and Couscous 105
Lunches 37
Mango Lime Coconut Rice 30
Maple Bacon Fry Bread 84
Maple Nut Oatmeal..26
Margarita Cheesecake...118
McMountain Breakfast Sandwich 36
Menu Planning...9
Mexicalli Hummus..47
Mexican Coffee Mix 20
Miso Mushroom Soup...66
Mocha Almond Breakfast Shake 17
Mocha Mousse Pie 116
Morning Gorp 48
Mount Daniel Wrap..40
Mushroom Tomato Rice 85
Mushrooms Paprikash...101
Oatmeal
    Apple Cinnamon Oatmeal......................................28
    Carrot Cake Oatmeal 27
    Maple Nut Oatmeal..26
    Pina Colada Oatmeal...28

Obi's Salad..62
Orange Spice Coffee Mix 21
Orange Teriyaki Chicken and Rice 92
Oyster Veggie Leek Stew...69
Oysters
    Oyster Veggie Leek Stew..69
    Oysters and Rice 88
Oysters and Rice 88
Pancakes
    Double Almond Pancakes 32
    Peanut Butter Pancakes...31
Pasta
    Creamy Pesto Noodles with Veggies.................................101
    Creamy Salmon Carbonara 100
    Eagle Creek Stroganoff...98
    Mushrooms Paprikash 101
    Pasta ala Squatch..102
    Pasta Morena..97
    Pasta with Creamy Mushroom Sauce 99
Pasta ala Squatch 102
Pasta Morena..97
Pasta with Creamy Mushroom Sauce......................................99
Peachy Green Iced Tea 19
Peanut Butter Banana Pancakes 31
Pickle Gulch Apricot Bites..51
Pina Colada Oatmeal 28
Potatoes
    Cheesy Black Bean Mashed Potatoes.................................82
    Chili Cheese Mashed Potatoes 82
    Ginger Coconut Rice and Sweet Potatoes..........................96
    Lemon Paprika Mashed Potatoes 83
    Oyster Veggie Leek Stew..69
    Potato Egg Scramble 35
    Spicy Potatoes and Tomatoes 86
Pretty in Pink 33
Queets Valley Shepherd's Pie..107

Quinoa
American River Sunshine Salad 61
Backpacker's Quinoa Soup...70
Chicken Curry Quinoa Salad..63
Tomato Herb Quinoa 85
Ramen...77
Bacon Mushroom Ramen 80
Beef Stroganoff Ramen 79
Chicken Ramen Soup..77
Coconut Curry Chicken Ramen..78
Lemon Dill Tuna Ramen 78
Rice
Banana Rice Pudding 113
Black Beans and Rice 94
Chicken Almandine 93
Ginger Coconut Rice and Sweet Potatoes...............................96
Greek Chicken and Rice...88
Green Tea Rice and Vegetables..95
Lemon Dill Tuna and Rice 89
Lemongrass and Ginger Rice with Salmon 90
Mango Lime Coconut Rice...30
Mushroom Tomato Rice 85
Orange Teriyaki Chicken and Rice 92
Oysters and Rice 88
Rice and Veggies with Peanut Sauce.......................................95
Thai Mango Chicken and Rice...91
Rice and Veggies with Peanut Sauce 95
S'mores 123
Salads..57
American River Sunshine Salad 61
Black Bean and Corn Salad 64
Dilly Tuna Salad 59
It's in the Bag Trail Salad 58
Lentil Bulgur Salad..62
Obi's Salad 62
Unstuffed Tomato Salad 58

White Bean and Fennel Salad..60
Salmon
    Citrus Lentils with Salmon...108
    Creamy Salmon Carbonara 100
    Lemongrass and Ginger Rice with Salmon 90
    Obi's Salad...62
Seattle Wrap..40
Sesame Peanut Bites 55
Smoothie...16
    Coconut Ginger Smoothie 16
    Creamsicle Smoothie 17
    Mocha Almond Breakfast Shake 17
Snacks and Trail Mixes...48
Soup
    Asian Mushroom Soup..76
    Herbed Vegetable Broth...72
    Miso Mushroom Soup...66
    Oyster Veggie Leek Stew..69
    Split Pea and Bacon Soup 68
    Tomato Basil Lentil 67
Southern Wrap...43
Spiced Pear Tart..121
Spicy Potatoes and Tomatoes..86
Splash's Fruit Bars 54
Split Pea and Bacon Soup 68
Springer Mountain Cooler 23
Strawberry Fields Forever 49
Sunshine on the Ridge Mix...50
Thai Mango Chicken and Rice 91
Thai Me Up Wrap..42
Toddler Mix...50
Tomato Basil Lentil Soup..67
Tomato Herb Quinoa 85
Tuna
    Dilly Tuna Salad 59
    Lemon Dill Tuna and Rice 89

Lemon Dill Tuna Ramen 78
Unstuffed Tomato Salad 58
Vanilla Green Tea Mousse 114
Vegetarian White Bean Chili ....·75
Veggie Dippers 128
Veggie Tofu Scramble 34
White Bean & Fennel Salad 60
White Blaze Salmon Dip 43
Wraps
    Athenos Wrap 41
    Cali Wrap 41
    Esmeralda Wrap...39
    Mount Daniel Wrap 40
    Pretty in Pink...33
    Seattle Wrap..40
    Southern Wrap 43
    Thai Me Up Wrap...42
X-Rated Lemonade 22

www.ingramcontent.com/pod-product-compliance
Lightning Source LLC
Chambersburg PA
CBHW022136080426
42734CB00006B/380